G000044770

Mike is that rare consultant whom we actually came to view as a vital team member. Over the years he has shared his expertise teaching and helping us to hire, qualify, manage, and develop our sales team, sales processes, and training platforms.

Harry Moulopoulos

Partner and Vice President of Sales, Packaging Solutions Inc.
Milwaukee, Wisconsin

Mike Carroll is much more than a sales coach—his work has had a massive impact on our entire company and on me as a leader. Mike has been instrumental in helping us build our sales leadership team and a sales infrastructure that has helped us grow revenue at a level we never thought possible. With Mike's guidance, we continue to make incremental improvements that drive top- and bottom-line growth. If you are serious about scaling your business, listen to what Mike says, and you'll be on your way.

Greg Rosenblatt

Chief Operating Officer, Stark Carpet
New York, New York

Mike's no-nonsense approach to leadership has helped us to build a solid foundation for our sales management team. Focused on coaching, accountability, and motivation, our team now lives and works "above the line."

Rhonda Rockwell
Director of Sales, Strategic Financial Solutions
Buffalo, New York

In *The Sales Team You Deserve*, Mike Carroll presents CEOs with a single question: Are you willing to become the best? If you are, then you have a single choice: pick up this book—and a pen—and begin following Mike's advice, clearly described in the pages that follow, straight away. Look, everyone deserves a great sales team, but it's only those who are willing to work for it that will earn a great sales team. It's time to get to work.

Bo Brustkern
Cofounder and CEO, LendIt Fintech
Denver, Colorado

Mike Carroll has been working with us since 2017 to build up our core strength in sales. Just like in physical fitness, without core strength goals cannot be achieved due to unexpected injury or ongoing pain that prevents success at the highest level. Core strength in sales means hiring the right person considering your markets and growth plans. Mike has worked closely with my company to support us in defining the right sales methodology and the right sales professional profiles given our sales cycle and typical deal size. Mike has coached our VP of sales on the hiring process, worked with us to select and customize a CRM that fits our markets, and has provided a consistent sales coaching approach across the organization, including how to have difficult conversations with customers, implementing price increases, and identifying different types of decision makers. Results show consistent revenue growth, and his experience has been invaluable to our success.

Holly Bellmund
President and Chief Operating Officer, GLC Minerals

Just as athletes use great athletic coaches to achieve their best, entrepreneurs partnered with a great business coach can definitely achieve more. Mike Carroll overachieved during his multi-year coaching engagement with Electromate. He challenged our experienced sales team to raise their game to a higher level and, under his tutelage, they delivered. This is a lot easier said than done when dealing with seasoned sales professionals selling complex high technology robotics. I rank Mike a first-class coach in the specialized area of sales process and methodology and would recommend him without any hesitation.

Warren Osak
CEO, Electromate Inc.
Toronto, Ontario, Canada

Mike was instrumental as a sales coach and trainer to both my sales team and me as its sales leader. He instilled strategic thinking, discipline, and accountability among the team and offered me wisdom, support, and guidance to be a better leader. Thanks to his inspiration, we've grown our team, and I've been able to hire a real sales leader—something all CEOs should strive for. I highly recommend reading his words of wisdom in this book!

Ken Wolf
CEO, Revelwood
Florham Park, New Jersey

Our company has worked with Intelligent Conversations for several years. Through his consulting practice and this book, Mike does a terrific job of taking complex sales team development challenges and breaking them down into understandable concepts and action items. He succinctly explains the impact organizational dynamics have on sales, as well as how to develop individual sales professionals. It is a quick read that stimulated a self-assessment of things we may be doing that hold us back from reaching our true sales potential.

Loren Semler
President, Semler Industries
Franklin Park, Illinois

Ten years ago, Mike worked with my company to develop a process for understanding our customer needs and refining that into a service offering. Mike's practical and straightforward advice is a road map to success. From hiring to making the decisions of when to let poorly performing employees or unprofitable customers go, *The Sales Team You Deserve* is the definitive playbook for smart CEOs to build a world-class sales team.

Kirsti Tcherkoyan
CEO, 20/20 Insights
San Francisco, California

Years ago, I was introduced to Mike Carroll via a client reengaging following the firing of their assigned salesperson. We discussed the situation, and asked why in their eyes had our salesperson not worked for them. "That's why right there," the client said. "They never asked me about and/or researched my business to have a constructive conversation. It was always about 'catching lunch.'" After asking a few more questions and having in-depth conversation, they shared how they were transforming their prior ineffective sales team experience and suggested we engage with Mike's company, Intelligent Conversations.

All the steps for success outlined in Mike's book, *The Sales Team You Deserve*, clearly defined why I was good at sales, but also why my sales hiring and development programs were not working. The total sales experience from hiring to development to success is a process, and Mike does a great job of laying it out and explaining why, if followed, you can improve your team.

Jeff Zeman
President and owner, Zeman Technologies
Waukesha, Wisconsin

Mike is always on point. He has a deep understanding of what it takes to build a great sales team, and this book is an insightful look at how to approach this process methodically and deliberately.

Eric Naaman
President, Damotech
Montreal, Quebec, Canada

Mike Carroll is one of the most sought-after sales subject matter experts in the country. His expertise from assessments to delivery and design of sales development programs as well as sales coaching is second to none. Our company has worked with Mike and his team and has had great success. One of the amazing things that Mike can do is to extract assessment results and deliver a custom program specific to client needs. So often in the world of sales training and coaching things can get canned and mundane—not with Mike. He's an absolute joy to work with and someone I would recommend to any sales organization that's not just simply having problems with sales but that also wants to take their sales to the next level. There is no one better than Mike and Intelligent Conversations.

Tim Hagen
CEO, Progress Coaching
Milwaukee, Wisconsin

Great salespeople and teams don't happen by accident. This book is a must-read to help you transform your sales team.

Molly Fletcher
CEO, The Molly Fletcher Company
Atlanta, Georgia

There are a tremendous number of books on selling and far fewer on leading sales teams. With few noteworthy exceptions, you can skip most of the books in these two niches and not have missed out on a single revelation. Mike Carroll's book is the exception to the rule. Mike deftly blends data, best practices, and some important lessons to deliver a modern blueprint to develop the sales team you deserve. Don't skip Mike's book, because it contains a recipe that is just right.

Dave Kurlan

CEO, Objective Management Group
Boston, Massachusetts

Mike Carroll gets it. Whether you think you know why your company is not achieving your sales targets or just can't figure out what's missing, this book will show you precisely what you need to do. Mike's methodology is clear, simple, and will deliver results. Every time. But it will take some work. If it is important to consistently attain your sales targets, then follow the path detailed in the following pages. Read and implement what is in this book, and let your sales sail.

Les Rubenovitch

President, Winning Edge Consultants
Toronto, Ontario, Canada

The Sales Team you Deserve is a must-read for any CEO or leader who is struggling to build a high performing sales team. Mike Carroll is one of the good ones. He is a master at cutting through the BS and getting to the core issues and solving them. When I started my business, I had never sold a thing but was thrust into the world of having to sell my service to feed my family. After years of struggles, I attended a workshop that Mike was presenting. I was amazed at the transformation I experienced from that one workshop. I then hired Mike as my sales coach, and he single-handedly solved my sales gap. Today I approach sales with a confidence I never knew I could have. If you need to sharpen your sales skill and/or build a high performing sales team, read this book next weekend. You will be so glad you did.

Keith Upkes

Business growth coach, Keith Upkes Coaching
Success Lead, Metronome United
Vancouver, Washington

The Sales Team You Deserve flies in the face of what we've been taught about achieving sales success. Mike has been coaching sales teams for close to twenty years; he's one of the best, and the content of his book is a must-read to create a strong sales team with a practical step-by-step approach.

Cléo Maheux

Cléo Maheux, Inc.
Montreal, Quebec, Canada

The Sales Team You Deserve is an eye-opening, powerful, and instructive book for CEOs. Mike Carroll hits the bullseye with his understanding of salespeople, sales processes, and sales management practices and how to apply them—once and for all—to upgrade your selling organization to become the one that you deserve. If you run an organization and feel like your salesforce isn't producing what you need, read this book.

Mark E. Green

Founder and President, Performance Dynamics Group
Author, Activators: A CEO's Guide to Clearer Thinking and Getting Things Done *and* Creating a Culture of Accountability
Speaker and business and leadership growth coach to CEOs and executive teams
Union Hall, Virginia

As the CEO of a publicly-traded B2B company, I would live and die by our quarterly numbers and reporting those out to our shareholders. As much scrutiny as I was subject to, I don't feel I had the same visibility into the black box of our sales team. I wish I had read Mike's book then! He is able to get right to the heart of the matter and demystify sales for any CEO. Mike is a true sales professional, coach, and teacher. His clear and relatable style translates into actionable steps to begin implementing into your business. I highly recommend Mike's book. Read it today and begin building the sales team you deserve tomorrow!

Glen Dall
Business coach and advisor, Apex North Coaching
Minneapolis, Minnesota

Mike's the real deal. In this book, he's used his years of experience and hard data to clearly define exactly why you might not have the sales team you want, what's stopping you fixing that, and then how to fix it through a clear road map to follow.

Brad Giles
Owner, Evolution Partners
Author, Made to Thrive: The Five Roles to Evolve Beyond Your Leadership Comfort Zone
Perth, Australia

Mike has done a great job of giving CEOs a holistic road map that is a realistic depiction of what it will take to help their business supercharge growth over multiple revenue plateaus.

Alex P. Bartholomaus
President and CEO, People Stretch Solutions
Washington, DC

Read this book!

I've been coached by Mike Carroll, and he's my go-to sales resource whenever one of my coaching clients has a sales challenge. I love that in this book Mike doesn't take the traditional approach of outlining some "magical" new sales process. He understands that it's not just about process; it's about building a great sales team. Thank you, Mike, for writing this book!

Mike Goldman
Owner, Performance Breakthrough
Business coach, author, and speaker
Paramus, New Jersey

I have worked with Mike Carroll and watched him coach people (including myself) for years. Mike has provided a solid prescription for your organization's sales issues. His holistic approach of not just technique, but also mindsets and behaviors, gets to the root of sales challenges. Mike provides a step-by-step way to evaluate your sales team, its leadership, and all the attributes that go with having a successful sales organization. Mike has nailed the issues and has practical solutions to those issues. This is one of the best books on organizational sales that I have seen in a long time.

Michael Mirau
Founder and Chief Business Strategist, ProActive Leadership Group
Dallas, Texas

What Mike Carroll lays out in this book is exactly what growth-minded CEOs who are looking to increase sales need. The steps laid out in *The Sales Team You Deserve* will create the momentum-changing attitudes, sales processes, rhythms, and outcomes that high-performing sales organizations are made of. You're reading from an expert who has the experience and insights to help you grow—period. Enjoy this book and take action. You won't regret it!

Ryan Groth
CEO, Sales Transformation Group
Maui, Hawaii

I have known Mike Carroll for more than twelve years. We first met when I was in charge of evaluating and training a twenty-three-person salesforce, of various backgrounds and abilities, for a major ready-mixed concrete company in Chicago.

Unable to accomplish this daunting task by myself, I brought in Mike and his program to help us meet our goals. The principles in his new book, *The Sales Team You Deserve*, delineate the key formulas we used to improve performance and increase profit margins by more than 10 percent.

I was so impressed with Mike's talent and his system that upon retirement I began working with Mike as a sales accountability coach. One hundred clients later, I can say with complete confidence that Mike's program delivers!

Jack Madderom
General Manager of Sales and Marketing, Prairie Materials
Chicago, Illinois

Read this book, apply the concepts inside, and watch your company grow. Mike's methodologies work—period! I have worked with Mike as my coach while at several companies I've led, and the results speak for themselves. As CMO and EVP of business development, I used Mike's coaching and input to grow that company by a 49 percent CAGR (compound annual growth rate) for twelve years running. We started at $10 million in annual revenue and grew to $1.2 billion. I then went on to become the CEO of a healthcare start-up, and with Mike as my coach I was able to grow that company from zero to $20 million in less than three years. Currently I am the president of a telecom services company, and last year, relying heavily on Mike's methodologies and concepts, we grew from $62 million to $93 million with strong margins. Please enjoy reading this book, and be sure to put these ideas into action—you'll be glad you did.

Scott Pickett
President, GTH
Dallas, Texas

Mike provides a real-world perspective to CEOs on how to build and lead a high-performing sales team. Mike's strength is in working with a sales team to expand their capabilities through sales coaching that goes far beyond the tips and techniques you would find in a normal sales training program. As a CEO, I value his development-based approach to creating a sales culture based on accountability in a way that will serve my company for the long term. His work with me and our team has been a cornerstone in our year-over-year revenue growth, as evidenced by the numerous times we received recognition for being among the top 50 growing companies in our region. Having worked with Mike for several years, I've benefitted from his compendium of sales knowledge, from situational advice on winning a big deal to building a strategic sales process while expanding our team. In *The Sales Team You Deserve*, Mike brings to the page his many years of experience and time-proven approach to sales team development using the same positive and people-oriented philosophy you experience when working with Mike in person, in a very readable, casual style that makes the content relatable and actionable.

Michael Andre
President and CEO, Gateway Ticketing Systems, Inc.

Mike Carroll has been instrumental in helping us develop a culture of continuous improvement as part of our Sales Talent Offense strategy. Our previous sales training as well as our approach to implementing new processes and technologies wasn't getting the results we needed. Mike's data-driven approach helped us understand where we need to focus to improve our results. He then helped us implement a coaching framework to develop our sales team while improving our ability to execute our sales processes. Mike's common sense, practical approach has helped us grow revenue by over 35 percent, and we continue to make progress.

Brad Fischer
Vice President, Experitec, Inc.
Lenexa, Kansas

This book reads like Mike Carroll talks: direct, no-nonsense, actionable, and results-driven. I have seen Mike's sales team development processes work in four organizations over the past twelve years, and I can attest that his data-driven sales road map process works for CEOs, sales managers, sales teams, and sales leaders. *The Sales Team You Deserve* is a clear, concise, easily understandable road map to help you grow your sales team and build your sales engine into productive, predictable, humming sixteen-cylinder perfection. The processes shared here are proven, and they deliver appealing, reliable, and predictable outcomes. Mike's latest book is full of ideas and wisdom that produce game-changing sales results. All you must do is embrace them, follow them, and apply them with discipline. Ready to do that? Then let's get going!

Ron Huntington

Legendary business coach, Gazelles International Coaches; Gravitas Premium Coaches; Metronome United Growth Coaches; Executive Mentors and Trainers Seattle, Washington

THE
SALES
TEAM
YOU DESERVE

MIKE CARROLL

THE

SALES

TEAM

YOU DESERVE

Why CEOs Tolerate Mediocrity and
What YOU Can Do About It

Printed in the United States of America.
Library of Congress Control Number:
ISBN: 978-0-578-38432-0

Cover Design: David Taylor.
Layout Design: Wesley Strickland.

*For my wife Pam, whose consistent love, encouragement,
and support makes all the difference. And for our children
Madeleine, Julianna, Catherine, and Benjamin for giving me
a reason to work so hard and for sharing many years of joy,
laughter, and occasional silliness. I love you all.*

CONTENTS

ACKNOWLEDGMENTS

I AM TRULY BLESSED. I have had the good fortune of working with some smart people over the years and, as a result, there are more people who have impacted me along life's way than I can possibly list in this short format. Let me pause to acknowledge everyone I've worked with, everyone I've done business with, and the many coaches and colleagues I've had the pleasure of learning and collaborating with over the years. Thank you so much. I have grown from my interactions with each of you. And please forgive me for not individually recognizing you.

I would be remiss if I didn't celebrate the influence of a few special individuals who helped me with this project and along my journey as a business owner. Alex Bartholomaus, Frederic Lucas, and I have been meeting as a peer group every other week since early 2012. Without their encouragement I'm not sure this book would have gotten off the ground. Mark Green, Brad Giles, and Keith Cupp were all kind enough to read early drafts and provide the feedback I needed to hear to make this book better. Tim Hagen's boundless energy, creative thinking, and passion for Sunday night pizza meetings have made me a better coach and business owner. Scott Pickett and I have had every possible combination of business relationship—he sold to me when I worked at a large regional bank, we were colleagues on the leadership team at a software start up, I have provided sales coaching to him and his sales teams at a couple different stops along his career, and through it all we have built an amazing friendship. And finally, Keith Upkes has been there for more years than either of us would care to admit, pushing me, challenging my thinking, helping me reframe things to get out of my own way, and telling me what I need to hear to keep growing. Thank you all. I could not have written this book or built my sales consultancy without your support and friendship. I am truly blessed.

FOREWORD

IN THE FALL of 2003 I had the honor of being invited to spend an hour with Dr. Stephen Covey, author of *The Seven Habits of Highly Effective People*, along with seven other executives and senior sales members from our business development team. As the vice president of sales and marketing for a software company, I listened intently as Dr. Covey shared the principles of his seven habits through a rich set of stories from his life of learning, often through his family interactions. *Begin with the end in mind* continues to be one of my favorites of the seven habits. It requires both vision for the future and a tangible measurement of what the end looks like to be successful.

In this book, *The Sales Team You Deserve,* Mike Carroll leverages the principle of beginning with the end in mind to answer the most compelling and recurring question in the mind of CEOs: "Why can't our company produce consistent, profitable sales results over a longer span of time?" What might taking your sales function to the next level look like? Here is what Mike has found over his two decades of sales experience:

- *Higher quality* opportunities entering into your sales pipeline
- *Speed of movement* of opportunities through the sales pipeline
- *Fewer but higher probability* of closable proposals and winnable quotes
- *Increased winning ratio* of proposals to deals closed
- *Optimized sales efficiency* of the ratio of deal profit margin to selling expense

The interesting aspect of Mike's insights in *The Sales Team You Deserve* is that the principles are *simple* but not *easy* to apply and enjoy. Why? Most CEOs do not demand a systematic approach to building their sales function based on science (data), experience (wisdom), and development (coaching and training). In this book, Mike delivers all three, and he elegantly captures and communicates his sales success algorithm to achieve consistent sales success, often with mid-market companies that have longer and/or more complex sales cycles. What are the key elements in achieving this success?

- Assessing and then hiring the right sales talent
- Developing your sales talent through systematic coaching
- Building a highly effective, repeatable, scalable sales process
- Selecting and using the right systems and effective measurements in sales
- Creating a successful partnership between marketing and sales

I have known Mike Carroll for a decade at the release of this, his first book, *The Sales Team You Deserve.* I and some of our colleagues in Gravitas Impact (Mark Green, Mike Goldman, Adam Siegel) have asked Mike several times, "Why don't you write a book Mike? You have so much to offer and need to get your message out to CEOs and sales leaders!" At last, it is here! It will be hard to find a better man, a more experienced sales development expert, or more insightful topline Sherpa than Mike Carroll to help you design, build, and coach your company to consistent, profitable, long-term sales results.

Keith Cupp

Founder and CEO, Gravitas Impact Premium Coaches

HOW MOST CEOS WILL READ THIS BOOK

IF YOU ARE like many CEOs we work with, you want results right now. Let me help you out. Go to page 155, the beginning of chapter 8, and take the survey. There are three questions for each topic in this book that will immediately help you understand where you need to focus your time, energy, and attention to get the sales team you deserve. Then go to whichever chapter speaks to your weakest point (or your greatest opportunity for growth) and start there. Of course, if you are not the kind of person who flips to the end of a PowerPoint to see the recommendation without hearing all the details, please feel free to read this book like a normal person. Enjoy!

INTRODUCTION

BY PICKING UP this book, you're joining the hundreds of business owners, CEOs, and senior executives I've worked with since starting my company in 2004. Like them, you're probably frustrated with your sales team at some level. Maybe you're *very* frustrated, or maybe you're just quietly annoyed. And no matter what you tell your investors, your board of directors, or your buddies at your CEO roundtable, deep down inside, you know you do *not* have the sales team you deserve.

It's embarrassing. You invested in sales training. You hired and fired sales VPs. You installed new customer relationship management (CRM) systems. You invested more than you care to admit into marketing and lead generation programs. And you hired recruiters who promised to stack your team with A-players. And yet year after year, your sales team produces mixed results. You exceed plan some years, but do you know why? Can you repeat it? Did you grow enough? Could you have grown more? But then other years, you come up short. Again, do you know why? Even when your salespeople seem to be doing everything right—they make the right calls, add great opportunities to the pipeline, qualify the budget and approval process for each opportunity, ask for the business—you lose the deal (again).

It's maddening. Opportunities you expect to close somehow evaporate. Deals you've written off suddenly close out of nowhere. Your sales forecast should be the single most accurate predictor of future revenue in your company, yet it almost never is. (By the way, isn't it amazing how many deals move to "next month" around the twenty-fifth of the current month?) Sometimes, it seems there's no correlation between your sales team's focus and what actually happens. It's not like that in other areas of your business. If there's a problem in accounting, production, or shipping, you can usually fix it pretty quickly. But a problem in sales? Where do you start?

This book isn't about teaching you some new breakthrough sales process or secret technique. It's about understanding what's getting in the way of having the sales team you deserve.

I'm glad you asked, because you can start with this book, and it's different from most books you might turn to when you have problems with sales. This book isn't about teaching you some new breakthrough sales process or secret technique. It's about understanding what's getting in the way of having the sales team you deserve and then implementing systems and processes to help you get it.

In these pages, I'll share with you the road map I've used with hundreds of companies to transform their sales organization and help business owners and CEOs get the sales team they deserve. At my company, Intelligent Conversations, we work mostly with companies that have annual revenue between $20 million and $200 million. We've certainly worked with smaller companies, and we've worked with some very large companies (for example, American Express and Bank of America). With that in mind, the road map I'll share is designed for small- and medium-size businesses (or SMBs) and lower-middle-market companies.[1]

To clarify further, our consulting practice focuses on working with business-to-business (B2B) companies that have a direct sales team. Since that type of organization represents the majority of our experience, the ideas and approaches I share in this book are best suited for this type of company. That said, we have also successfully applied these approaches to companies that use distributors, sales rep firms, or other channels. And we have successfully helped companies with a business-to-consumer sales focus (we even worked with a retail jewelry operation once). The road map I'll share in this book is calibrated for B2B sales organizations. That means this approach is bested suited for sales organizations that tend to focus on large opportunities with a longer sales cycle that requires salespeople to navigate through a fairly complex, multiparty buying process. Frankly, the more complexity in your sales process, the greater the impact this road map can have.

If what you've just read doesn't describe your business, don't worry. I'm confident you'll still gather valuable nuggets in this book

---

1   Within each chapter we share examples and additional information, either a relevant client story or data to illustrate the point we are making. Maintaining our client's confidentiality is very important to us, so we have refrained from using specific company names, we have changed the names of the individuals in our examples, and in some cases, we have masked industry-specific information to protect the identity of the people and clients we serve. While the stories and examples we share are based directly on our real experiences, in some cases we combined situations or modified the story for brevity and to better illustrate the principles we are reviewing. The results we share in terms of revenue growth or other impacts are all based on real-world outcomes we have helped our clients achieve.

that you can apply to improve your sales situation. However, if the description fits your business perfectly, then buckle up—we're going to help unpack all the elements you need to get right to have the sales team you truly deserve!

Let's Start with Data

I'm grateful for my relationship with Objective Management Group, Inc. (OMG) for many reasons. We've been consistent, award-winning partners for years, and OMG has won awards regularly over the years for having the best sales evaluation tool on the market. I'm particularly grateful for the access we have to incredible data from OMG that helps identify the key attributes for high-performing salespeople, sales leaders, and sales teams. OMG has been gathering data on salespeople for more than thirty years, and let me tell you, it is *not* pretty.

We'll get into more detail on that subject when we get to chapter 5 and discuss the single most important thing you can do to get the sales team you deserve (which is to evaluate your sales team), but for now, let's just focus on a few shocking statistics (based on evaluations OMG has run on more than 2.1 million salespeople over the past thirty years) that reveal a basic fact: most salespeople are not that good![2]

---

2   Unless otherwise noted, all data in what follows can be attributed to Objective Management Group. To explore their statistics, please visit http://stats.objectivemanagement.com/220.

SALES PERCENTILE

■ Elite ■ Strong ■ Servicable ■ Weak

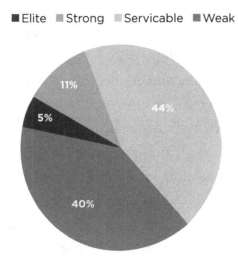

11%

5%

44%

40%

SELLING SKILLS

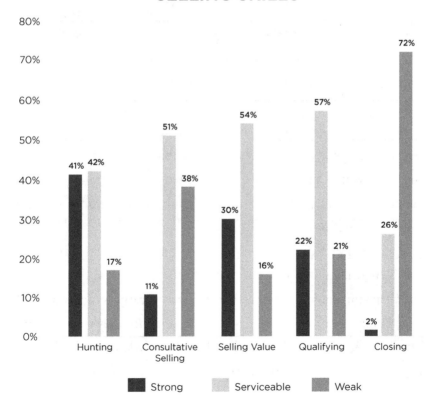

	Hunting	Consultative Selling	Selling Value	Qualifying	Closing
Strong	41%	11%	30%	22%	2%
Serviceable	42%	51%	54%	57%	26%
Weak	17%	38%	16%	21%	72%

■ Strong ■ Serviceable ■ Weak

One reason you don't have the sales team you deserve is probably that most of the salespeople you've hired over the years are just not that good. By the way, the goal isn't to hire a team of elite salespeople because these high performers can often be quite disruptive to your business and culture. Instead, I coach CEOs to think more about shifting everyone up a bit, meaning you make your serviceable salespeople strong and your strong salespeople even stronger. Focus on making consistent, incremental progress over time (every month, quarter, and year) so you can look at your sales team and say, "Wow, we're getting better. We're having better conversations, pursuing better opportunities, selling at high margins, reducing our sales cycle, improving the accuracy of our forecast, making better hiring decisions, and onboarding new salespeople more efficiently and effectively."

However, the problem goes beyond having salespeople who just aren't that good. Making this problem even worse, OMG's data shows that sales managers don't invest enough time coaching their teams, and when they do coach, sales managers are having the wrong conversations and aren't very effective at it besides. Finally, the data shows that most companies have *not* defined a consistent, milestone-centric sales process. I joke with CEOs that if you have ten salespeople on your team, you have at least fifteen different sales processes because, depending on the day, you might have people on your team who use several processes.

Here's the thing: in our experience, most salespeople and sales managers really do know what to do. Many even know *how* to do it, but they still don't do it consistently. They clearly understand and might even agree with the techniques and tactics they've picked up when you have invested in sales training, but when they find themselves in a live sales situation, they freeze up and can't execute. That's what's so maddening. And sales leaders fall into the same trap—they understand that they should do more coaching and develop their sales team, but when you look at what your sales leaders actually do with their time, it becomes really clear that they spend most of it doing everything except coaching and developing their team. That's why I wrote this book. In this book, I will help you identify the obstacles that keep you from having the sales team you deserve and then show you the way to get it.

My Journey as a Salesperson

In hindsight, I guess it was inevitable that I'd end up in sales. My father, Paul Carroll, was a brilliant engineer who designed and sold paper machines. Both of his brothers (my Uncle Bill and my Uncle Jack) were also in sales. Grampa Carroll (their dad) talked about "the Carroll hustle gene," which I inherited, apparently (and I'm pleased that my four kids seem to have it too).

I went to the University of Wisconsin, and while there, I started a T-shirt business and hawked funny, sometimes offensive T-shirts outside of Camp Randall Stadium. Talk about immediate market feedback! I quickly learned what sold (and what didn't), how asking questions and building rapport increased sales, and how getting to the stadium and setting up early made all the difference (location, location, location!). I graduated with a degree in English literature (not engineering) and promptly moved to Chicago, where I started my career as a copywriter at a small marketing firm. It became pretty apparent that although I had solid writing skills, my true talent was in talking with prospective customers. I moved from the creative side to the account side and moved through a couple of larger ad agencies. I then left the agency world and went into banking, where

I worked as a product manager in commercial banking and focused my attention on launching internet banking solutions for commercial, small business, and retail customers. I did a brief and ill-fated stint at a dot-com start-up right before the bubble burst in 2000. Talk about bad timing! My last real job involved selling software to banks and managing a data center where we hosted hundreds of internet banking and e-commerce applications for banking clients. The common thread through this phase of my career was that I loved building things, I loved selling new ideas and products to customers, and I loved being a change agent. I'm grateful for the experiences I gained working in lots of different corporate environments, both large and small. I'm grateful for the opportunities I had to work with smart CEOs and senior executives as I pursued new markets or launched new technologies, and I'm grateful for the start-up experience and the friendships I made and still enjoy to this day. All of these experiences in the first phase of my career (1990–2004) set me up for success in my consulting practice at Intelligent Conversations.

I left corporate America to start my consulting practice in 2004. I had only one contract (with American Express), and it had a tight deadline. It was a nerve-racking time, but within the first month, I was fully booked and have not looked back since then. My initial emphasis was on market development programs focusing on generating qualified leads for commercial bankers (a group of salespeople who will do anything they can to avoid making cold calls). I got great results but quickly learned that these programs failed two out of three times. That would be a great batting average in baseball, but it's not so good as a sustainable business model. As I studied the differences between the programs that worked and the programs that failed, a few clear patterns emerged. The winning programs had a strong culture of accountability and salespeople who were coachable and would adjust and adapt to get results (rather than firing the consultant).

I discovered Objective Management Group while studying these programs and quickly appreciated the power of their data-driven approach to measuring sales teams. Working with our clients to do a thorough analysis of their sales team and measure all of their deficiencies helped us understand exactly why our market development programs failed two out of three times. I started taking this data-driven approach as a way to qualify (or disqualify) potential customers for my lead-generation programs. And as I got into it, I became fascinated with helping teams unlock their potential and drive massive improvements. Since shifting our focus from market development programs to sales force transformation programs, we've worked with hundreds of sales teams across different markets who sell different products or services to different buyers, with different levels of competition and different price points, and in different economies. Through these engagements and across this range of experiences, I again noticed some clear patterns—this time about what it takes to build a high-performing sales team that can dominate your market. This book uses all of that knowledge, insight, and experience to help you build such a team.

You *can* have the sales team you deserve, and in these pages, I'll share with you the road map to get there. Let's get started!

CHAPTER 1

WHY CEOS CAN'T SOLVE SALES ISSUES

CEOS WITH UNDERPERFORMING sales teams typically can't solve the issues on their own. Why? Mostly it's because CEOs generally aren't natural salespeople and usually have backgrounds outside of sales. Because of this, they see sales through the filter of what they did before becoming CEO and are uncomfortable and unfamiliar with what it takes to build a successful sales team. They don't know what to expect from their teams, they don't know what "good" looks like, and frankly, they don't know what they don't know. But they *do* know that their sales teams should be better. They can be passive about it and hope it gets better, or they apply what they do know from their backgrounds to try to improve their sales teams. But neither of these approaches works very well.

As uncomfortable as CEOs might be with trying to figure out what's gone wrong, they can't run and hide from the problem. CEOs must be personally involved in sales efforts—even if they're an engineer, an attorney, an operations person, or have a marketing background—because their focus and attention will either lift or destroy the sales team's morale. But more importantly, CEOs have equity in their title. The three little letters behind their names really give them a lot of clout and power that they can use if they get directly involved. CEOs shouldn't abuse their clout, and they shouldn't become salespeople, but they can use their title and its clout strategically. When a CEO makes a phone call or joins an important sales meeting to support the salesperson, it conveys how seriously they are taking the opportunity and the importance of winning the prospect's business. In many cases, a well-timed call from the CEO can break a logjam and get an opportunity moving again. And they don't have to give up all of their time but just commit to a little bit of their time and lead from out front.

The CEO Background Filter

CEOs must recognize that their experiences and background influence how they view their entire business. In other words, they have a background filter that affects where they put their focus, what they are most comfortable doing, and how they interact with the various functions throughout their company (including sales). Most come from one or more of the five most common paths to CEO: operations, finance, marketing, sales, and legal. Sometimes they're from another part of the business, particularly if they're a founding CEO who started their company because they were passionate

CEOs must recognize that their experiences and background influence how they view their entire business.

about whatever it is they do. Those CEOs tend to be more hands-on and have an operational focus. Let's look at how CEOs views of sales can differ depending on their background filters.

- A former plant manager with a hands-on operational background might try to make sales a process like a workflow on the manufacturing floor or in a design process. It's not necessarily wrong, but it's just one model.

- A CEO who was in finance sees everything through expense management and dollars and cents (salespeople as an expense and not a revenue source). Investments in coaching, development, and training seem like unnecessary expenses, and their whole mindset is about cost reduction and minimizing expenses rather than opening up the throttle and growing.

- Another CEO who grew up in marketing probably has more market awareness and is more customer-focused and customer-facing. But CEOs who drive sales from that perspective tend to be all about the new product and the presentation. They'll have beautiful collateral and complicated, beautiful presentations, but they can skip over the fundamentals like needs analyses and digging into prospective customers' issues.

- Even a CEO who comes from sales has a blind spot created from their experience in selling that might be outdated or in a different marketplace. The assumption is that what worked for him ten or twenty years ago should work today. But techniques and concepts from the late 1980s and early '90s are out of place today.

- A CEO with a legal background can also be operationally focused and too mired in details. A lawyer-turned-CEO can be all about risk mitigation. Salespeople might bend the rules a bit to find ways to make their product fit and solve a problem it wasn't designed to solve. Legally minded CEOs think, "That's not in our contract; that's not a specified use." Their quotes and contracts tend to be more complex, and these things drive salespeople nuts.

For some CEOs, sales is a necessary evil or something that has to happen, but again, their natural comfort zone is usually in areas other than sales. Sales is a blind spot—they don't know what they don't know, and one thing they don't know is why they have a problem. And one of the things they really don't know, thanks to their background filters, is what a good sales team looks like.

What a "Good" Sales Team Looks Like

When I work with CEOs, I poke and prod at several topics and issues to get to why they can't solve the problem alone. "Tell me about your growth," I say. "How are you growing? Are you selling directly? How's your sales team performing?" I often hear mixed reviews of the sales team's performance—they have good years and bad years, they're growing at a pretty good clip, or, "We grow, but not everybody's hitting their numbers."

So I poke and prod some more. "How are your margins? Are you growing because you're discounting too much? Who are your best clients, and who's comfortable calling them?" The CEO quickly realizes that he doesn't know what he doesn't know.

Then I dig into the sales leadership. Some companies have salespeople but no sales manager, and the CEO is the default sales manager. If that's the case, I ask how much time she invests with the sales team. The answer is often "Very little. They come to me with questions or if they need me, but if they're hitting their numbers, I don't bother them."

Sometimes the CEO tells me he just promoted one of the salespeople to sales manager, and I find that he probably took his best performing salesperson and made her sales manager. This usually ends up a disaster because the skills required to be an effective manager are very different from the skills that made that person effective at sales. Maybe the CEO invested money in a sales manager, a sales VP, or a director of sales, so then I ask, "Well, how's that person doing? Where's their focus?" Often, the CEO tolerates a sales manager who's acting as a productive salesperson and isn't really coaching and developing the team.

These are just a few of a whole host of issues that show how a CEO typically doesn't know what "good" looks like. From our experience, this is what "good" means and what a CEO should expect:

- A high-performing sales team should have a sales leader focusing on coaching and developing the team so that every month, every quarter, and every year, you can see the team getting better.

- The sales team should be having better conversations with clients.

- You should be winning your proposals at a higher ratio.

- You should see sales growing and selling at higher margins.

- The handoffs internally to operations or other departments should be very smooth.

When I say these things to CEOs, I'm often met with a blank stare: "That's nothing like what we have." I ask questions about how much time the sales manager spends coaching the team, and the CEO doesn't know the answer. When I ask which team members are capable of selling at a higher margin, again, no answer. Then I ask, "How effective are you at spotting and hiring really good sales talent?" They get weak in the knees and don't have the answer. They'll say, "It's a crapshoot at best."

The problems remain unsolved, the CEOs don't know what they don't know, and they're simply tolerating things in the sales department that they wouldn't tolerate elsewhere, including other areas of their lives. They wouldn't send their kids to a mediocre school, for example. I ask them to consider if they're tolerating things in sales that they wouldn't think of tolerating when it comes to other departments' performance. If the shipping manager said, "We can account for 93 percent of the packages we shipped last month," the CEO won't celebrate but will probably ask, "Where's the 7 percent we lost? How's that affecting those customers?" If the CFO says, "Hey, I can account for 98 percent of our revenue," you can bet the CEO will want to know exactly what happened to that missing 2 percent. Where did that go? Yet, when the VP of sales says, "Hey, we're at 92 percent of plan," companies literally throw parties and celebrate. "We hit our plan! We had a stretch goal, guys. 92 percent—let's do better, but let's go out and celebrate."

Wow.

Typically, they want to have the best in all areas of their lives, yet they put up with a mediocre sales team. Why? Because they don't know what "good" looks like. Here are the steps you need to take if you want the sales team you deserve.

1. Decide to Become the Best

This is the commitment part: CEOs must decide to be the best and overcome any obstacles to being the best. To do this, you have to do three things.

• Recognize Your Own CEO Filter

You must recognize that your own CEO filter affects how you view your sales organization. Accept that your background might influence you or that you haven't been investing enough time or focus on sales, and that has to change. CEOs have to recognize their own sins in the current situation, and that's hard. Helping them recognize their sins and the impact they're having on sales results is one of the more difficult parts of the work I do with CEOs.

• Recognize Your Loyalty to Noncontributors

You have good people on your sales team—you know their kids' names, you've seen the kids grow up, and you have an enviable amount of loyalty to those people and their families. But if people on your team aren't achieving results or contributing their fair share, you have to ask yourself if you can find other roles for them. You can't make them be something they're not. Committing to being the best might involve looking objectively at everyone without letting your personal relationships cloud your judgment. Reset your expectations about the team. If they're not contributing in this role, find them another role or free up their future. You won't be telling them something they don't already know, and it's often a relief for them when you give them the opportunity to exit with dignity and grace (and a severance package that recognizes their loyalty). And they'll probably be grateful for it.

- **Commit to Doing Whatever It Takes**

  It can take a lot to get the sales team you deserve, and that's why you need full commitment to making the changes it will take. The changes outlined here are what many companies need to do to develop high-performing sales teams. The rest of the chapters cover more details on these steps.

2. Hire Stronger Salespeople

Hiring stronger salespeople is crucial to getting the sales team you deserve. In my experience, the fastest path to revenue growth is getting stronger salespeople on your team. Not only will they help you in your market, they'll also elevate the performance of your existing team. Building a system that allows you to constantly monitor the market so you can quickly upgrade your sales team when a strong salesperson becomes available is key to having the sales team you deserve.

3. Hire Stronger Sales Leaders

Sales leadership is where the rubber meets the road, yet most sales leaders have never been taught how to be a sales manager. They're winging it—honestly, they're winging it! They do their best—some are good, some are okay, but some don't have a clue. Both you and your sales leaders need to raise your expectations. Start by hiring people who are good leaders, but equip all sales leaders with the tools and processes to be highly effective, and change how they interact with their team. Give them structured frameworks so they can create a culture of accountability and have productive coaching conversations, unlock the things that get in their team's way, and make everyone incrementally better so that wherever they are on the continuum (good, bad, or lousy), they're *all* moving up the ladder. (Please see the box starting on page 83 in chapter 4 to see data on how ineffective sales managers are when it comes to coaching salespeople to higher performance levels.)

4. Let Go of Unprofitable Customers

Many companies hang on to customers that really aren't good fits for many different reasons. Revenue and margin are the obvious ones, but there are many more reasons, and you need to reexamine all of them. You might like working with a customer or their culture fits with yours, but it's not enough to keep them if you're losing money on them. Get clear about what makes great customers and be intentional when defining your ideal client profiles because your salespeople will take whatever comes their way, whatever is easy to close. Figure out who's going to help you grow (and get more of those clients) and who's holding you back (and take them off your books). Once you let go of unprofitable customers, keep your sales team focused on your ideal clients (and that means saying "no" to less than ideal clients).

5. Let Salespeople Go

CEOs often keep salespeople who aren't coachable or trainable, don't have a lot of development potential, and aren't hitting their numbers. Why? Let's go back to the topic of loyalty to noncontributors. Once again, find another role for that person where they can add value or free up their future. If they are coachable and trainable and they're hitting their numbers, ask how much more effective could they be, but be realistic. Sometimes you have to let the low performers go and hire people who are better than your top producer—that's where you really start to move the lever.

6. Change Your Process

In many companies, the sales process consists of finding people who might buy and then giving them a quote, and there's no in between. Salespeople will quote anyone who takes their meeting, and often they skip all the necessary steps along the way that ensure a good fit. If your process is like this, it needs to change. Have a thorough discovery process to qualify your prospects fully—not just the budget and the contract terms, but also the timeline and acceptance of what your solution can and cannot do.

CHANGE THE PROCESS TO CHANGE YOUR RESULTS

Over the years, we have worked with several manufacturers, including small job shops that produce metal parts and components for original equipment manufacturers (OEMs) and other customers. Sometimes our greatest strength can create blind spots that ultimately become a weakness. One CEO we worked with, Dave, was brilliant at organizing the workflow through his shop. Dave had an ability to see every inefficiency and could quickly configure and reconfigure his manufacturing floor to optimize throughput. Dave's manufacturing floor was producing with efficiency, but he was growing frustrated with his quoting department. The good news was they were getting more requests for proposals (RFPs) and requests for quotes (RFQs) than they could handle—they literally could not keep up with the demand from prospective customers.

What did Dave do? He applied his greatest strength (his operational mindset) to the problem and hired more quoters. He focused on key metrics like quote turnaround time and quote backlog. He calculated the number of quotes each team member should be able to produce per day, spent time focusing on building quoting templates, divided the work among different team members, added a quality review step, and sent quotes out the door with ruthless efficiency. Basically, Dave applied the same methodology he would use when solving a throughput problem on his manufacturing floor. And still, his frustration grew as their expenses went up but their business remained flat. He hired us to help address why they were losing so many quotes.

What did we do when we started working with them? We investigated their discovery and qualification process. We then looked at their win rate and learned they were only winning one out of every eight quotes they produced. If they were playing baseball, their batting average would be .125—not exactly Hall of Fame numbers! Working with the leadership team, we revamped their entire sales process and increased the rigor in their discovery and qualification process.

Within two months, the quality of their sales conversations improved, the number of quotes produced was cut in half, and they won a little more than half the time. In other words, their costs went down and their revenue went up. Instead of producing eight quotes to win one job, they could send out four highly qualified quotes to win two jobs. And their margins went up! In the eighteen months we worked with this client, their revenue went up more than 60 percent, and their margins went up about 25 percent.

This is a great example of a CEO getting in their own way and not having the sales team they deserve. Dave did not realize he had a blind spot that caused him to rely on what has always worked for him (improving operational efficiency and increasing throughput) instead of focusing on the quality of the sales conversations his salespeople were having. When we analyzed all the RFPs and RFQs and had the team call these prospective clients, we learned that in many cases the clients requesting quotes were supplying defense contractors who needed to show that they met a minimum bid requirement before awarding any work. In many cases, Dave's company never had a chance to win the business; they were just the third quote in a bidding process that required at least three quotes for every project. By making a few small changes in the sales process—such as improving the discovery and qualification process to disqualify opportunities that are not real—we had a massive impact on both revenue and profit margin.

7. Change Your Compensation Plan

Compensation plans are always a sensitive topic. If the plan is too generous (and salespeople have made too much money for too long), a change is problematic because everyone will leave. The CEO can't afford that and sticks with the plan, which becomes more ingrained. With a strong hiring process, you can build a pipeline of strong salespeople, change the comp plan when they come on board, and give the current team a transition period. Conversely, if your comp plan is inadequate (and salespeople are woefully underpaid), don't wonder why your turnover in sales is so high. Salespeople need an opportunity to earn. Commission-only plans tend to attract the wrong kind of salespeople. I'm a big fan of uncapped commissions and a base salary that keeps salespeople comfortable, but not too comfortable. Salespeople who aren't stressing about making their mortgage payment probably won't become too aggressive, but they shouldn't be able to join the country club, buy a nice car, and send their kids to private school on their base salary. Give them the opportunity to earn all those things with an uncapped variable pay component, whether it's bonuses or commission, because they should have upside. And you should be smiling when you write that check. You want your salesperson to be the highest paid person in the company, and if you've designed the comp plan right, that means that the whole company's growing.

8. Hire Outside Expertise

Successfully executing everything I outlined above on your own is a tall order. You can do it, but you will get there more quickly if you hire an outside expert. A CEO client once said to me in frustration,

"Mike, I tell you every time you're here that you're repeating things I tell the team, and they listen to you but won't listen to me."

I said, "This is what I do, and I'm the outside authority. You're their boss." Even though this particular CEO is a good salesperson— a great one, in fact—and she knows what to do, she sometimes struggles to explain how to do it to other people. She's far from alone in this. Helping people change is my profession, I've been doing it for years, and I'm good at it. I'm responsible for giving them information that's easy to consume and to adjust my methods to their environment, market, selling profile, and sales cycle. I've seen hundreds of situations while this CEO knows only what works for her (which might not work for everybody else). She lacks the background and ability that I have to adjust, adapt, modify, and make methods fit her team or each individual on the team and needs outside help. Whether you work with me or another sales coach, hiring an outside expert will accelerate change in your sales organization.

How CEOs Get the Sales Team They Deserve

The sections you just read cover the types of problems we at Intelligent Conversations deal with every day in working with companies to improve sales team performance. Here, I'm going to outline the basics of how we fix these problems when we consult with a company and scale that process for you in the rest of the chapters. Reading this book will take you down the right path if you choose to initiate changes on your own, and in the last chapter, I provide you with worksheets and other resources that you can access if you want to do that. Your other option, if you want greater impact and faster change, is to hire me (or someone like me). But this book will give you a game plan that you can at least try and will tell you if you need outside help.

Intelligent Conversations takes a data-driven approach in our engagements. We're more than just sales trainers and don't do one-size-fits-all training—we don't teach you "our" system but rather tailor a plan to your organization at multiple levels. Training won't be effective if we don't address all of your issues. And unlike sales training programs, ours all starts with data.

- Sales effectiveness and improvement analysis (SEIA): This is our first step when working with a sales organization. The SEIA is a comprehensive analysis of the people, systems, and strategies that affect revenue. It's the gold standard for sales evaluation, so we've built our business around this robust evaluation tool set.

- Set a benchmark. The assessment results set a benchmark, a starting point against which we can measure our effectiveness. Ten months to a year into a program, we'll run everyone through the assessment again and can empirically measure improvement and understand potential.

- Create a road map to get to the sales team you deserve. By analyzing the core attributes that get in the way of your team being change-ready and using data from the SEIA, we create a road map of what needs to be in place to effect the change you want.

- We lay a foundation first:

1. Evaluate the team (the SEIA).

2. Get them working on their self-limiting beliefs (for example, beliefs about money and how they frame questions). We're

working on their mindset and changing their belief system so they can implement what we teach them in a real selling situation.

3. Teach managers how to have the right kind of coaching conversations and establish a culture of accountability. We give them a structured coaching outline, not a script to follow. The outline is a framework they can adjust and adapt based on their style and their comfort zone.

4. Map out a sales process. It's amazing how few companies have mapped out a consistent, milestone-centric sales process. We put order and structure to the process without making it a straitjacket. By this time, we're usually three to four months into the process.

5. Sales messaging. We conduct a sales messaging workshop with a range of exercises to work on the language used to describe what your company does and how you serve people (a positioning statement).

6. Establish goals and territory plans. We look at where you're going to grow and how, along with many other factors (conversation, contact frequency, how many accounts each salesperson has, and so on). Companies establish such plans, but often they don't do it very effectively. Sometimes it takes an outsider like us to come in and give them different ways to look at it, different ways to analyze the data, and help them change how they approach it.

This process is the basis for the road map this book provides. Whether you create the road map and implement it yourself or with outside help, you need a strong commitment to doing it and the willingness to take the time it will take.

Time and Commitment

Fixing an underperforming sales team takes time and commitment, so don't look for a quick fix. Your issues developed over a long time, and it'll take a long time to get back on track. Your progress will be incremental (two steps forward and one step back), slow, and gradual, and you should expect a time frame of eighteen to twenty-four months before you start seeing real improvements. If you are frustrated by your current sales situation, you may be frustrated by this longer time frame.

Fixing an underperforming sales team takes time and commitment, so don't look for a quick fix.

Here's the deal—if you want results that will stick (unlike many sales seminars or quick programs where your team forgets everything they learned in two weeks), you need to make the commitment to stay the course. Most of our commitments are for at least six quarters. Typically, it takes about a month just to do the analysis, and from there the clock starts ticking. Commit to the following:

Expectation Management

You need realistic expectations about the time and commitment involved. Don't expect your situation to change overnight, and that's whether you're implementing steps for change or you hire someone like me or other outside expertise.

Hold Sales Leaders Accountable

Keep your team on track and hold them to it, and especially hold your sales leaders accountable. They're going to make excuses, push back, resist, or complain. A typical salesperson mindset is that they just want to go out and sell, and they want to know why they have to sit in this workshop, why they have to do an online program and coaching calls. They don't necessarily see the immediate benefits. At the extreme, some might even leave because of what you're doing. You must make it clear that you're committed to this and it isn't optional because you are committed to achieving results. You *must* follow through. You made a series of decisions that got you to where you are—you can't expect to make only a few changes and everything's going to be better. No, you have to work it back the other way, and that takes time.

Follow Through

The fix is an ongoing process. After implementing changes, you must follow up and reinforce. For example, my team won't just do a single workshop for a client because it wouldn't make everything suddenly change for the better. We've worked with some of our clients for eight or more years, and they keep us around because we keep adding value. (That's not every client, though. Usually, we try to get in and out, but some clients want to keep us around for reinforcement, so we'll do a workshop or other activity maybe once a quarter.)

How You Know It's Working

People always say to me, "Tell me about your success rates. Do you have any examples?" One of the things I love about being in sales is that it's very easy to measure your success or failure. But make sure to measure what's really going to show your progress from the big-picture view. Here's the thing: everybody wants to measure revenue. It makes sense, right? Well, revenue's a lagging indicator. Revenue happened in the past.

Suppose a CEO says to me, "Hey, Mike, you have to move revenue, and you have three months to do it. This report says it's going to be $3.6 million, and I want to see that in three months." That's not going to happen because it's not realistic. It won't happen in three months because it depends on the length of your sales cycle. Most of our clients sell large-ticket products and services through a complex, multiparty buying process with long lead times (three to six months is typical, though it'll happen faster in a highly transactional business). In a six-month sales cycle, a call made today is working on deals six months later in a best-case scenario.

Given the nature of our programs and that incremental change is happening over six or eight quarters, it's clear that revenue is *not* the only or best indicator. The first area to monitor as you begin to implement this road map is the quality, quantity, and movement of opportunities in your sales pipeline. Put your focus on the new opportunities your sales team adds to the sales pipeline (are they the right customers, talking at the right level, focused on the right products and services?); the quantity of opportunities your sales team adds to the sales pipeline (more is not necessarily better, focus on getting enough of the right opportunities in the sales funnel); and as you monitor the quality and quantity of new opportunities, watch what happens next (are they moving to the next step in your sales process in a timely manner?).

Consider this: in our programs, it takes us six months to get our systems installed. Then it takes another three months for the team to start using it consistently and sales leaders to reinforce it consistently (so now we're nine months in), and then the team starts having better conversations, adding better deals to their sales pipeline, pursuing better opportunities with better messaging, having more qualified deals, and winning more quotes. Then add on the sales cycle (let's say six months), so you're at month fourteen or fifteen at least before those deals that entered your pipeline in month nine start to close. Absolutely, we should measure progress by revenue, but the revenue is probably going to show up right around the time I'm leaving.

I've had CEOs say to me later, "You know what? Our best year was the year right after you left." So I describe to them the timeline I just stated, and then it makes sense to them. Yes, measure me by the impact we have on revenue growth—please hold me accountable to that. But when we conducted the sales effectiveness and improvement analysis, we set benchmarks based on what the analysis found and agreed on a handful of *leading* indicators to measure months down the road. This will give you a more precise picture of how well (or not) you're doing in your transformation.

Identify some leading indicators to give you confidence that your transformation is working. Here are some good indicators that are realistic:

- Improved quality and quantity of opportunities entering the pipeline

- Those opportunities moving through the pipeline more consistently from one milestone to the next (deals you would normally leave in there longer are being disqualified and moved out of the pipeline sooner)

- Better quality of quotes and proposals (fewer quotes going out because you're disqualifying them sooner—and that's okay because you don't need as many quoting resources and will actually start winning more)

- Winning a higher number of quotes per those sent out (ratio)

These are just a few examples of good leading indicators, and you can come up with others. Sometimes it's as simple as keeping track of your team's calendar for several weeks to track how many appointments are set up, and then go back in two months and look at their calendars again. But watch your team for signs that can't necessarily be measured but rather observed: your team's conversations getting better, your managers having better conversations with the team and having a better impact on them, your customer expectations improving, and things starting to go more positively.

I've tried to capture a formula in this book, sort of a template that we use to help transform sales organizations. If you do nothing else but read this book and begin to apply it, you should see progress. You can pick and choose some of these concepts and ideas and start to implement them in the format I'm sharing without necessarily needing an outside consultant like Intelligent Conversations. But if you want to accelerate that progress, we can help you. This is what we do.

Questions for Reflection

1. How does your background—your career path and experiences—shape your perspective of and interaction with the sales function in your company? What are your potential blind spots when it comes to sales?

2. List a few actions you can take to leverage your title to become more involved in the sales function in your company. For example, calling past customers, meeting with prospective customers, speaking at events to drive leads for your sales team, etc.

3. Are you settling? If you could improve one thing about your sales organization, what would you pick and why?

CHAPTER 2

DEFINING SUCCESS AND SETTING GOALS

MOST COMPANIES WE WORK WITH already have a pretty good handle on setting company goals. Some are certainly better than others, but generally speaking, there are plenty of planning models available for companies that want to set annual and quarterly goals—whether you use the 7 Attributes of Agile Growth, the 3-Year Highly Achievable Goal (3HAG), the Entrepreneurial Operating System (EOS), or the One-Page Strategic Plan (OPSP). Likewise, many sales organizations take the same approach and will develop annual sales goals and then break those down to quarterly sales targets. And of course, these targets may vary from company to company depending on their industry, typical sales cycle, any seasonality they may experience, their mix of products and services, the markets they serve, and a number of other factors.

Success and the markers for success are different for every company because every CEO and company faces different challenges. "Success" might even change within a single organization from one year to the next—or even one quarter to the next—and often the target is a moving target. Many companies tend to start (and stop) the process of defining success and goal setting at the company level and work down. We like to flip that model and work from the bottom up by having managers invest the time to lead each team member through a personal goals exercise and then help their team member align their personal goals with the work they do at their company. When salespeople (and other team members) begin to see your company as the means through which they can achieve something that is personally meaningful to them, that's when the magic happens. People will work a lot harder for *their* goals versus an esoteric company goal, like improving EBITA by *x* percent.

People will work a lot harder for *their* goals versus an esoteric company goal.

Teaching sales managers to create a culture of accountability through an individual goals program is one of the core things we do at Intelligent Conversations. The feedback we get from clients shows that creating a goals program probably had the biggest impact of all the changes they made. When a manager leads a team through a personal goals exercise, it can be a transformational moment. Your sales team is made up of many individuals, both salespeople and managers. Defining success for your team starts with the individual. As the sales organization becomes more successful—driving revenue growth for you—a well-designed compensation plan should help them make more money too.

Success for Individual Salespeople

Defining success for individual salespeople and creating goals that lead to success has to be done differently for each person because of their own unique challenges and goals. It's important to understand what motivates each person. You must help salespeople identify what success looks like in their personal lives to define success within the company.

I think about this from two perspectives. Certainly, from a business perspective, everybody has an individual sales goal that involves Mr. or Ms. Sales Rep owning a portion of the sales plan. But to even reach that point, I want the sales manager to really understand the individual—the person. When a manager invests time in leading the team through a personal goals exercise, it shows the team that their manager actually cares about the team and about each salesperson as a *person*, not just a cog in the machine. The sales manager is saying to them, "We actually want to know what's important to you because work is about more than just work—it's about *why* you're working." When sales managers understand why each salesperson is working, it becomes easier to hold them accountable. It's always easier to hold them accountable to something that matters deeply to them.

What does each person on the sales team care about? Why are they working so hard? Maybe they want to send their kids to a private high school or private college, they want to buy a bigger house or save more for retirement, or they want to provide their aging parents with additional in-home care. Maybe they want a new bass boat. Their goals could relate to health or fitness—they want to have more time to work out at the gym to drop twenty pounds and have more energy to play with their kids. Why each person works (the goals) is very personal and different for each person. Their goals mean something to them, and that's what sales managers need to know because this is the salesperson's internal motivation that will get them to perform at their best.

In our program at Intelligent Conversations, we take sales managers through a personal goals exercise, and it's transformative for them. But then we have them lead their teams through that same personal goals exercise. The objective of that is twofold: to communicate with salespeople that you care about each one as a person and then to connect their goals back to job performance.

Communicating that you care about each person is also a team-building factor that helps solidify a team. The manager says to the salesperson, "I actually care about you as a person. I care about your goal and helping you to reach it." But you also communicate accountability. "I'm also going to hold you accountable to that goal. So if you want to lose twenty pounds, save more for retirement, or buy a bigger house or a cottage or boat or whatever, I'm going to hold you to that."

The magic happens when that manager can take that personal goal and then connect it back to what it means in terms of job performance and what that person needs to do to reach their personal goal. It's a bit more straightforward if the sales role is commission based. Say the person's goal is to send their daughter to a private high school with tuition of $16,000 a year. The question to that person is: How many more sales do you need to make to reach that goal? The two can then map out how to do that. The sales manager then holds that person accountable to reaching the goal, which is something that's more important to that person than some impersonal company goal. It's far less meaningful to a salesperson to say, "The ownership team wants to improve EBITDA by two-tenths of a percent this quarter, so we all have to sell at a higher margin." Holding someone to a personal goal empowers that person to be their best—the best possible version of themselves. And if that version is someone who can comfortably send their kids to private high schools, then holding them accountable means they need to make sure they're producing at a level where they can easily afford to do it and still have all the other aspects of their life that they enjoy.

Now we come back to the business perspective. Every manager has to map out sets of goals for everyone on their team. I like having a handful of goals and think that three or four is about right, and I like quarterly goals. You can set goals for whatever time frame you want, but with a ninety-day time frame, you'll measure progress over thirteen weeks in a quarter. However, the three or four goals aren't all personal goals. They can't be, or you're ignoring the business needs. I like to have three business goals and one personal goal.

Typically, I coach sales leaders to think in categories. Sales managers and salespeople will usually set goals around net new business or new accounts acquired. So how many new customers does a salesperson need? That number's going to depend on what you sell, the length of your sales cycle, and the size of your average contract value. We have clients with nine-month sales cycles and some with very large deals, so a goal of one new account per quarter might not be realistic unless you've had them in your pipeline since three quarters ago. If your business is a very transactional one, your goal might be one account per week. You have to set a new account goal based on your sales cycle and other factors like that.

Often, there's an expansion goal. You already have accounts landed, so what else can you sell to them? Do you have other products or services that you can offer that maybe those accounts don't know about or haven't bought yet? What's your game plan to go get them using all of your services? Maybe you get many orders from one division in the company, so now you can think about how to get customers from another group or division. It might not apply to you, but it's something worth exploring.

I also like to include a learning goal, which helps improve the whole team, especially if you can fill gaps in skill sets. Think about what new skill or knowledge base each salesperson could acquire in a quarter that would make that individual a better sales professional. It could be something related to sales, products, or even going into another market space. A sales learner goal, for example, could be closing skills. Maybe the person has lots of opportunities in the pipeline but isn't closing them. You can focus on what's getting in their way from a closing perspective and have that person work on honing their closing skills. If it's moving into a new market space, you set the learner goal and then provide some resources so they can do their research on that market. In any case, the sales manager will coach them through that learning process to reach the goal.

Sometimes our clients want to focus on addressing an issue that's more specific to their business, like a need to improve margins or stop discounting. One of our clients was selling in a very competitive space, and their customers often have thirty-six- to sixty-month contracts that they can't get out of, so they spend lots of time talking to people who are in no position to buy. We had them focus on a goal of identifying every week at least two firm dates when an account had a contract expiring—even if it was in three years—and then you know you can influence decisions if you start talking with them six to nine months before their contract expires.

Those are just some examples of business-specific goals you might set, but that said, if you can work with just these four goals—personal goal, new account goal, account expansion goal, and learning goal—and nothing else, your team will be very focused and in good shape.

Transformation happens when the manager invests the time to really lead their team through that process from a personal goal perspective and then hold them accountable and connect. When a sales manager can talk with a salesperson and get them to see the company as the means through which they can achieve their personal goal, magic happens. Then the new account, expansion, and learning goals all fall into place because you're basing all of them off helping each person achieve a personal goal. I even think that *every* manager should know the personal goals of everyone on their team, not just sales managers.

Success for Sales Managers

Success for sales managers is different because the manager's job is to motivate the sales team and keep everyone on track. They must not only manage the numbers, but also the people driving those numbers. Sales managers should have a personal goal, just like each person on the team. The sales VP should have the same personal goal-setting conversation with sales managers that the manager has with team members and similarly holding the manager accountable for their own goal. Beyond that, for sales managers, I try to avoid goals (and compensation) centered on revenue. Even though I want a salesperson accountable for net new accounts closed per month or per quarter and accounts expanded and revenue generated, I focus on measuring managers and sales leaders by what percentage of their teams are achieving their goals. Although many people in this position have the word "manager" in their job title, we teach them to think of themselves as sales coaches rather than sales managers. A key concept is that we want them to manage agreements with their salespeople and then coach them when they fall short. By setting these types of goals, you're saying, "You *must* manage agreements with your team members and then coach them to succeed." Your team may be crushing it from a revenue perspective, but if only two of your people are really performing and everyone else is behind plan, to me, that manager is failing, and the CEO is going to start asking questions.

Let's look at that situation more closely. Is this team performing and hitting? The team number might be achieved, but it's really two high-performing salespeople who are carrying everyone. Then the question is: Does the manager have anything to do with that or is that manager just lucky to have two really high-performing people on the team? In this case, I focus on what kind of conversations the manager is having with the team and whether they're the right frequency, for example, and I look at how well the manager is coaching the individuals, if any coaching is taking place. Again, these are factors related to how that manager is managing the people.

What other factors relate to managing the team and contribute to the team achieving their goals? Some examples include:

- Coaching. Managers should have consistent weekly coaching conversations with everyone on the team.

- Availability. The manager should be available to the team when they need managerial support.

- Supporting sales, not doing sales. Some managers will step in and close deals for the team when they should be supporting them and teaching them how to close deals themselves.

That last one is very common. Managers who used to be salespeople tend to have a natural instinct to go get the kill when they can get it. We see this quite often. When they do that, they actually stunt the growth of the team below them, and it's demotivating to the team. Salespeople can think, "Why do I even try when the manager is just going to come get the deal and take all the credit?"

Measure managers based on the outcomes their team produces and what percentage of the team is performing rather than just raw numbers. I think many CEOs, particularly if coming from an operations or finance perspective, tend to not care what the team's doing as long as they're hitting their numbers. But you have to dig in a little bit and see what's behind that. Ask what percentage of the team is achieving their goal (and it would be hard to hit 100 percent) and then ask what needs to change.

A strong sales manager is a force multiplier because they will help each sales team member make incremental progress and produce more than they would on their own.

A strong sales manager is a force multiplier because they will help each sales team member make incremental progress and produce more than they would on their own. How do you get the sales team you deserve? You hire a strong sales manager who can help your average salespeople become good, your good salespeople become great, and your great salespeople become even better.

THE POWER OF HELPING YOUR SALESPEOPLE SET MEANINGFUL PERSONAL GOALS

Here are two short stories about the power of understanding the *personal* goals of each salesperson on your team. First up is Katie, a top producing salesperson at a growing software company. The CEO, a woman named Sarah, was also functioning as the sales manager for this five-person sales team. Sarah was very skeptical when I explained that we wanted each team member to compete a personal goals exercise but agreed to go through with it. I think she was surprised by the results when she discovered Katie's personal "why" and unlocked her full sales potential.

Katie was a single mom with two small boys. Through the goals exercise, Sarah learned that even though Katie, her top producing salesperson, was making $150,000 or more per year, she had not learned to manage her money very well (this is actually quite common among high-performing salespeople). Katie was embarrassed that she still lived in an apartment complex. She shared, "I worry about the impact on my two little boys—they are seeing and hearing things on the weekends that I would prefer they didn't know." Her dream goal was to buy a house, but it seemed impossible. Sarah sat down with Katie and helped her identify which neighborhood she wanted to live in. She then helped Katie develop a plan to save 20 percent for the down payment and showed her how she would save money once she switched from paying rent to paying her mortgage. Then Sarah looked at Katie's sales activity and showed her how a few very achievable changes—increasing the number of net new meetings, focusing on including a few additional services with each new contract, and closing more deals—could put her in position to buy her new house within nine months. Once Katie understood *exactly* what she needed to accomplish to hit her personal goal of buying a house, she was unstoppable. She hit the accelerator and purchased her first house within five months of that conversation with Sarah. Katie kept her foot on the gas, and three months later, she had all new hardwood floors installed. Every day when she walks into her house and across those beautiful hardwood floors, she is reminded of the conversation Sarah had with her and remains an extremely motivated employee.

A similar story brings us to Andy, an inside sales representative for a building materials company. Andy's goal was to be able to coach his son's Little League team. This would require him to leave early three to four days per week between April and June. Andy's manager Nancy was not sure how to accomplish this, but together they set a sales goal that front-loaded Andy's activities during the first quarter. They figured if he were ahead of sales plan by the start of the Little League season in mid-April, he could comfortably leave early a few days each week to organize team practices and coach the games. Nancy and Andy set a go/no-go goal for the end of February—if he was not at a certain revenue level by that date, he would need to tell his son that he couldn't coach the team.

Once Andy understood *exactly* what he needed to produce to reach his goal so he could coach his son's Little League team, he absolutely crushed it. Not only was he ahead by the end of February, he stayed ahead all year (even when he was leaving early to go coach during the season). Andy was absolutely blown away by Nancy's commitment to helping him achieve his goal and her tenacity in holding him accountable to hit the agreed upon results.

When you invest the time to understand the personal "why" of each salesperson on your team and then help them understand exactly what they need to accomplish to achieve that goal, awesome results will follow.

Success at the Company Level

Success at the company level means looking beyond revenue alone, even though increasing revenue is the overall goal for every company. Revenue is a lagging, unclear indicator and is only part of the definition of success. The main benefit is consistent, predictable sales and a much higher confidence in the sales forecast. When CEOs and executive leadership teams can look at the sales funnel and know with a high degree of certainty that the sales function in their business will produce reliable, consistent results like the other functions in their business, they can make better decisions.

Our clients want to know what results our programs produce, and, of course, they want to know about the revenue growth our clients have achieved. We have clients who were at $15 to $18 million in revenue when we started with them and two or three years later were at $45 to $50 million. As I mentioned earlier, CEOs will often tell me, "Our best year was the year after you left." Well, I don't take it personally because it's what I expect. If it takes us two quarters to get the right kind of changes in place and for people to apply the right kind of changes consistently (and salespeople are human and will take two steps forward and one step back), then the lag makes sense if you're measuring by revenue. So I want to look at some leading indicators, like adding the right number of opportunities to the sales forecast every month, calling on the right accounts instead of the comfortable and familiar accounts, and measuring movement through the process (which most companies can't do because they don't have a clearly defined sales process that's milestone-centric and can be investigated every step of the way).

CEOs need to keep an eye on the bigger picture and the broader aspects of the business. If they're watching only revenue, they might not notice changes, problems, or opportunities in the company or industry. The bigger picture helps you see how to identify and set company goals beyond the lagging indicator of revenue.

For example, we had a client who didn't want to grow their revenue but rather wanted to improve margins. So we didn't grow their revenue at all, but we did improve their margin significantly. It required them to have an entirely different type of conversation with customers. They had to sell higher-value product. They couldn't produce any more of it, so to grow, they had to change what they were selling and so changed the conversations they were having. They sold ready-mix concrete, a very low-margin product. (A yard of ready-mix concrete sold for about $70 per yard, so every ten-cubic-yard truck was worth $700 of revenue, of which the company might make $2 per yard, which translates to about $20 profit per truckload after expenses.)

We had to get the contractors who bought the product to think of that material differently. Instead of worrying about more yards sold, we thought about more revenue per yard of concrete poured. We changed the conversation by framing it in terms of how the contractors could free up some of their labor to be productive elsewhere on the job site. The process of pouring concrete can use up to four people, but we said, "What if we could show you a way that you wouldn't need four people? We can put fiber in the concrete to make it stronger, and then you can pour it with fewer people." That's the kind of conversation we teach them how to have, one that requires thinking creatively about the products and the customers' needs but gets you beyond thinking about only revenue and shows you other factors to use in company goal setting.

How does your company define success and identify goals? Companies generally identify their goals uniformly. Many executives open last year's budget spreadsheet, adjust the numbers to account for 5 to 15 percent growth across the board, resave the file with a new name, and mark "next year's budget" off of their checklists. They call this budget planning, and that's the extent of it. They hand the document to the sales manager, who usually divides the amount of the percentage increase by the number of salespeople on the team, then tells the team that everyone has to increase sales by x percentage more than the previous year (also known as each salesperson owning a portion of the sales plan). This is a fundamental problem of defining success because it ignores so many aspects of what success really is in the company's real world.

Most companies are pretty good at setting goals in concept—we want to grow at 20 percent, or we want to grow by a certain amount. You can sit in a boardroom and have a theoretical discussion about how much you want to grow, but can you actually sit down, map it out, and say, "*How* are we going to grow there? What are we going to sell? To whom will we sell it? At what margin? How are we dividing that out among the team?" The devil's in the details, and it can make a huge difference when a sales leader maps out their revenue plan from a *detailed* perspective, not just growing by a certain percentage or by revenue.

Looking at details, consider questions such as these:

- Have you defined your ideal client and the different entry points to get into those companies?

- Which clients can say, "I want to learn more about your products and services"?

- Who else at client companies cares about the problems you can solve (beyond the same kind of person your salespeople are targeting with the same kind of conversation)?

- What are the attributes of the types of businesses you want to sell to, what functional roles do you want to target within that business, and what messaging do you need to have to get to them?

As you start to answer those questions, the company-level goals become much, much clearer. It's not just about adding any revenue—just selling to anyone who will buy your product. Proactively focus your sales team and train them on those types of accounts. So a company goal might be not just to grow revenue by adds but to grow it the right way by focusing on those accounts. From this, you see a picture emerging of how to define success for the sales team as a whole, not just each individual.

Tips for Setting Team Goals

From the business perspective, companies also want to set team goals. Keep an eye on the bigger picture when doing this. It's okay to want to increase revenue, but when setting goals for the sales team as a whole, ask yourself *how* you want to achieve revenue growth. There are many ways to increase revenue, and you can set team goals from these strategies.

Diversify Deals

Some salespeople will focus only on closing the really big monster deal. If they hit their deals, they're going to crush it, but if they miss them, there's going to be a big hole in your budget. Other salespeople focus only on closing small deals. Focusing on only one size of deal is a mindset issue for salespeople. In most cases, they aren't told where to focus but rather "Here's your number—go get it," and they'll go after it in the way they feel most comfortable. As noted, this has limitations. Most companies have work to do in both directions and include focusing on medium deals. A good mix of deals from large to tiny is important. A team goal can be to reach a mix by varying the size of deals across the board. An entire team that's productive and working toward a revenue goal means not having to rely on the heavy hitters as much and worrying about the small deals being small.

Focus on Current Customers

The entire sales team should take a closer look at your current customers from a new perspective. Salespeople often stop selling and just take orders from regular customers because it's easy work. But what would happen if they went further and asked: What's happening with you? Why do you want what you're buying? What else do you need (if they've even thought about that)? Asking extra questions might lead to increased sales and discovering what other business problems the buyer has and who else in their company cares about them. Does this steady buyer even know about all of your company's services? The bigger deals could be right in front of your sales team if they just start asking questions, and expanding existing accounts is a great team goal.

Asking such questions won't always lead to sales, but it sometimes gives you a chance to build trust and loyalty in other ways. If you don't have a product or service that can solve their problem, just say so. Listening to the problems and trying to come up with solutions—even if that means admitting that you can't help—can show the customer that you care. Your honesty and authenticity can grow the company's credibility and increase your customers' trust in you, and that's worth a lot. Salespeople might fear losing their regular sales if they start asking a lot of questions, but the goal is to keep conversations open with your regulars at all times. You want to turn a transaction into a conversation whenever possible and approach customers from a broader perspective, not a narrow transactional perspective.

Revisit Former or Dormant Customers

Calling on former or dormant customers shouldn't be too hard because they've done business with you before. "Dormant" means something different in different companies. For example, a company on a six-month sales cycle might label a customer as dormant if they bought in the past but not in the last eighteen to thirty-six months. Anyone who hasn't bought in at least three years would be considered a past customer, and you would want to treat them as a new customer when trying to win their business again. The team's goal should be to conduct a highly focused campaign with these customers because it could churn up some orders and generate revenue. (You could even gain important intelligence about why they haven't been ordering.)

It's just a matter of reconnecting, and you'll be amazed how many times you'll get a positive response. It's almost like they forget about you if you don't keep on top of it. If you neglect prospecting and take your foot off the gas, you'll see it in your results. You have to keep going and constantly feed that pipeline.

Acquire New Customers

Your sales team should always be working on expanding your customer base, and exploring adjacent markets can open multiple revenue streams in the same market space. For example, a company selling cloud-based software that tracks hours for professional offices and specializes in one type of firm can look at customizing the same software for other professional firms (depending on the modifications and return on investment). Entering new markets, however, can requires understanding the new market's requirements and what it means for other departments in the company (like maybe changing and improving processes). Setting team goals around acquiring new customers involves the whole company for that reason.

A goals program for all involved is the first step in transforming for success. But what else can you do to help ensure success? The next chapter covers your team's environment and how you can optimize it for their success.

Questions for Reflection

1. How strong is your understanding of each team member's personal goals and how working at your company creates a path for achieving those goals? Do your managers have a good understanding of their team's personal goals?

2. Beyond revenue production, what other goals should you assign to your sales managers to drive performance and raise expectations for the entire sales organization?

3. What can you do to drive more discipline around tactical sales goals each quarter? Does everyone on your sales team have clarity around new customers to acquire (and leading indicators to measure that), account expansion, and account retention?

CHAPTER 3

CREATING AN ENVIRONMENT FOR SALES SUCCESS

CEOS NEED TO create the right environment to set the sales team up for success. Unfortunately, this is rare—often, the unique needs of the sales team are either not considered at all or are given only secondary consideration. Salespeople face challenges that don't concern anybody else in the company. Rules that make sense for team members who are in the office every day may not easily transfer to salespeople, who spend most of their days outside of the office. Technology decisions, systems requirements, policies on expenses, reporting requirements, the meeting rhythm, and many other policies and decisions made with the best intentions often have unintended consequences when applied to the sales organization.

To be clear, I'm not advocating a free-for-all where salespeople can get away with whatever they want. They still need to be accountable and produce results. All I'm suggesting is to take a look at your sales environment and ask: Is this policy or decision going to enable or prevent sales? Too often, we see sales environments that have evolved over time through a series of incremental decisions that seem perfectly reasonable on their own but cumulatively create lots of friction in the sales process. High-caliber salespeople aren't going to stick around if that's your situation. What are some of the common friction points?

From Sales Prevention to Sales Enablement

Sales enablement means providing the sales team with anything that helps align resources and actions to improve the company's overall sales effectiveness and helps support sales activities. Cultivating an environment of enablement starts with the CEO, who has to set the tone and get with everyone on the leadership team—every department head and every manager of the different functions in the company—and say, "First and foremost, we're a sales organization. Nothing happens until a sale happens, so find a way to support the sales team." Then the sales leader must be empowered to own that communication with other departments.

Sales support could be as simple as the marketing department coming up with templates, sales letters, and emails that salespeople can use. It ensures consistency, but it also saves the salesperson's time trying to create these things, and anything that eats into a salesperson's time is time wasted. Salespeople should focus on being in sales conversations instead of entering data into a database, trying to create a sales letter, arguing with accounting about travel expenses, or spending an inordinate amount of time doing market research on a prospect. They won't escape doing these things entirely, but putting tools, systems, and technologies in place to help make the team more effective enables them to be just that.

When we work with clients on creating environments that accelerate the sales process, I like them to look at several key sales factors to see if these things are working for them or against them in their companies.

- Technology: Make sure the sales team has the technology it needs to be effective.

- Travel policies: Be flexible and realistic with travel policy because salespeople spend a lot of time on the road.

- Consistent messaging: Create consistent messaging that speaks to the prospects and tells a story about what you do, and then make sure everyone is on the same page with that messaging.

- Marketing and sales alignment: Good market intelligence helps salespeople make plans for engaging clients without spending time doing basic research. Marketing can help develop lists of sales targets and provide key market intelligence.

- Other departments' alignment and cooperation: Legal, finance and credit, operations, and any other department that touches sales must be on board with supporting sales. All departments need to be open to collaboration and feedback.

Technology

I could write a whole book just on how companies waste money on technology. Salespeople don't *always* need to have the latest bells and whistles, but they do need to have enough good technology to do their jobs. Knowing what sales is all about and how your people go about their jobs is crucial to knowing what's necessary and what isn't.

Hardware is easy: salespeople need a light laptop or tablet that they can carry around easily, not the twelve-pound monstrous leftover laptop the guy in accounting decided he doesn't want. Until you spend time on the road selling like your sales force does, you have no idea what it's like to deal with things like this. Software is a different matter. I see companies make lots of mistakes and waste tons of money on software without really defining what they need.

By far, the biggest mistake I see is companies spending gobs of money on customer relationship management software, or CRMs, and not customizing it for themselves. You have to look at your needs and spend time finding the right solution for your organization instead of just buying what might be the popular software of the year (or month or week). Without doing this, you could end up spending a crazy amount of money for something that's not customized for your needs, and you could end up using maybe 5 percent of its capacity. That's not value for your investment. One of the most important things to consider with CRMs is ease of use. I've seen systems that salespeople don't even use because they're ridiculously complicated. They just want to get names and phone numbers and move on but find they have to fill out six screens of information before they can even open up an opportunity. Configuring your CRM can't be done in a vacuum—you must involve someone from the sales team who will use it and make sure what you get isn't just what marketing or

Take a Goldilocks approach to CRM: you don't want too much or too little—you want just enough.

operations would like. It has to revolve around your sales process and make sense for your needs.

Take a Goldilocks approach to CRM: you don't want too much or too little—you want just enough. Keep it lean and simple. Include enough information so that any salesperson can pick up that opportunity, including where you are in the process, what has happened so far, what the next step is, and so on. Having a clear milestone-centric sales process makes this easier because if everyone is following the same process and using a common language, it should be clear where each opportunity stands and what needs to happen next. Your CRM should reflect that process. Keep it simple.

Other useful technology tools are those to help share and manage content, particularly if you have a distributed sales organization with people in all corners of the country or around the world. A well-organized documentation system gives people the ability to look at past proposals and responses to RFPs or share templates and marketing materials easily. The upside to content management systems is that you can put thought into what you need to share and with which departments to share it and then set it up so that it works just the way you want it to. It's just a filing system, but one that anyone can access from anywhere.

You might also look at the many different virtual meeting platforms available. Companies that had already incorporated remote presentations and demos before the coronavirus disease (COVID-19) pandemic were in a better position to continue selling. Companies that relied on salespeople traveling around the country and meeting prospective clients face-to-face struggled a bit as they made the transition to virtual meetings. Salespeople who can master running effective remote meetings can be so much more efficient and will have a significant advantage over salespeople who don't adapt and continue to rely on face-to-face meetings.

Whatever technology you're considering, it pays to invest in the most current available if it fits your needs. Otherwise, you could end up needing to make another big investment sooner than you want to.

Flexible, Realistic Travel Policies

Salespeople travel for a good portion of their lives. Unfortunately, not everyone in a company understands what this means. I remember a salesperson who told me about his first face-to-face meeting with the controller who approved his expense reports. She looked at him and said, "So you're Jack. I would've thought you weighed about four hundred pounds from the kind of expenses you submit. How can you eat so much?"

He was stunned. Did this person who approves his expenses really not understand that when he's selling on the road, he's not the only one who's eating? Jack, like most salespeople, was taking customers and prospects out for business dinners, maybe occasionally pure entertainment, but this was all about relationships. Yet often, the perception is that salespeople are just out there having a good time. They're having steak dinners, going to basketball games, and doing a lot of things that, on paper—and if you don't understand what's going on when salespeople travel—looks like they're just having the time of their lives.

The reality is that sales is a very tough role, and I think people who haven't spent time on the road set travel policies that aren't necessarily attached to that reality. Your people are out there grinding for long hours every day, often traveling from one customer to another without coming home in between. Yet they have families and schedules outside of work that they're also trying to accommodate. They're living out of a suitcase, not seeing their family for long periods, and just putting their noses to the grindstone at all times while they're out there. In this reality, enabling success for your salespeople means being realistic and flexible with your travel policies and making sure that anyone in the company who touches travel understands fully what life is like on the road for your team.

I think one of the things that can drive good salespeople away is the little annoyances they can encounter when your travel policies nickel and dime them to death. If you're going to ask them to be away from their families and go from Atlanta to Detroit to Toledo, back to Detroit, out to Boston, out to Seattle, and then home, let them stay in a nicer hotel and have the little amenities that make that kind of travel schedule easier. Don't worry about the extra $150 a night at that nicer hotel. For busy, productive salespeople, something like a better hotel with amenities isn't just nice to have—it actually helps them be more effective. Along the same line, say your top salesperson is on the road from one city to the next for days on end but really wants to go home at some point for her daughter's soccer game. Understand that the extra $200 to get her on an earlier flight so she can do that won't break the bank, but it will go a long way toward fostering her loyalty and appreciation.

Of course, some salespeople will absolutely take advantage of flexibilities and try to push it. The bottom line is that it's a balancing act, so give your salespeople a certain amount of autonomy regarding travel, but you have to use good judgment.

Consistent Messaging

I mentioned that we conduct a whole series of workshops on consistent messaging because it's important to make sure that everyone is on the same page. We teach how to write positioning statements from the prospect's point of view, using a range of exercises to work on the language used to describe what your company does and how you serve people, and this sales messaging often turns into a sales playbook.

For example, when someone asks you what you do, you might respond, "I'm a commercial real estate executive." Well, that's more of a label. Saying that might make you feel good about your title, but you really haven't told that person a story about what you do. You haven't made your work relevant to his needs. We work on helping salespeople frame what their companies do in a way that immediately speaks to the client. The commercial real estate executive would be far more relevant to the client if he said, "I help office managers sort through available options for their expansion. I'm especially useful when they're feeling frustrated and want someone to guide them through that process." With a message like this that tells a story about how you solve others' problems, you're saying the same thing, but you've flipped it around and said it with the prospect in mind. It addresses their problems and what they want and need, and it will resonate with them.

I go through an example in the next section of how consistent messaging is applied with different emphasis depending on the role of the person with whom sales is engaging. It shows how the messaging isn't about the sales team or your company or even your solution, but rather it's about the customer and their problems.

Marketing and Sales Alignment

We see many companies spending plenty of money on market intelligence and marketing plans to generate sales leads. They'll buy directories or lists or information that are good resources for when salespeople are stuck and can't find information about a company they're about to call on. But I've seen a lot of marketing departments create materials, messaging, and lists that they think are relevant without ever consulting the sales team. They can do this without a solid plan for how to use the information, and sometimes they do it without really knowing who the company's ideal clients are. The marketing department can execute entire campaigns to generate leads, but they turn out to be the wrong kinds of leads. There's no alignment at all with sales, and it's crucial to have strong alignment between the sales VP and the marketing VP. Marketing must consider the sales team's needs. It's okay to test boundaries and push the envelope, but marketing also has to seek and incorporate real-world feedback from the field into what they do. If not, you're going to run into problems and will have to referee.

Planning must clearly define the ideal client, which roles sales should engage, and how to engage them with consistent messaging. First, it's important to be *very* clear about the who and the what: Who are your ideal clients, and what problems do they have that your company's products or services can solve? Determining this often involves departments outside of sales, and this is where the CEO's efforts to bring everyone on board with a sales-enabling mindset pays off. For example, identifying your target market might involve your finance team, which can assess target demographics by looking at your accounts' revenue and profit potential. They can tell you where you make money and which customers bring in recurring revenue versus one-time sales. Data like these can help you build a profile of your ideal client. What industries do they represent? Where do we start the conversation? What title or functional role do we add to the list? Where are we making the most money? This profile will help your marketing team build a list of targets that look like your ideal client, and those are the companies you should target.

The next level down, then, is: Who should our salespeople start conversations with at those companies? If you don't define that (and without a strong target list and a push), salespeople will call to their comfort level, avoiding situations where they're asked a question they don't know how to answer or where they're expected to punch above their weight. They'll sell stuff, they'll find a way in, and they'll close now and again, but if they're too comfortable, they might not really be talking with the right person. The real decision-maker might be a level or two above, and if they had started the conversation on a level or two above, well, think of how much more effective could they be. Your plan defines target companies that have problems you can solve and tells salespeople which person at each company is the ideal entry point, along with other people they need to talk with in the process (maybe two or three other roles).

Now you look at all of those roles from a messaging perspective—again, from the customer's point of view (and marketing helped you with this) because your messaging needs to be about them and their problems, not your solution (yet). Say you're selling software that helps companies do more effective financial forecasting and budgeting. You probably want to start talking with the CFO or the controller, who will have issues and challenges that you can solve. But at some point, you'll also want to talk with people further down the food chain who are doing reports in the accounting department, and you'll probably need to talk to some of their division managers or end users who consume the financial reporting that they put together.

You can describe the problem you solve, and you can emphasize different things depending on who you're engaging. The CFO wants to know about planning and forecasting, but a line accountant doesn't care about board presentations because he has fifty reports to produce every week, so your talk with that person involves how your tools can make him more efficient and take that report load off his plate. Then those who consume the reports—say they're division managers—want to know about how to tweak and customize those reports because standard reports are okay, but they really want to home in on one piece of information. This example shows how you can carry consistent messaging through various roles and hit each one's unique problems.

When your team can address all of these different roles with similar, consistent messaging that emphasizes different things according to the role they're engaging, that's when your company will really start to gain traction. Sales will start getting better opportunities in the pipeline, close them faster, and sell them at higher margins.

Other Departments' Cooperation

It can be very demoralizing when the sales team feels like it doesn't have the support of the rest of the company, and more often than not, that's how it is. From legal to finance to tech people, it's a two-way street on which departments need to agree to cooperate and align with sales, but sales has to hold up its end of the bargain too. The CEO has to make sure that all of this happens and set the tone across the board.

Getting your company's legal department into a sales-enabling mindset can be difficult because theirs tends to be risk averse. They look at every possible scenario that could cause harm and think of protecting the company in every circumstance, no matter how unlikely. It's an important function. But some businesses carry more risk than others do, so depending on your business, consider whether your legal approach is balanced. Are your lawyers looking for ways to say "yes" to salespeople and "yes" to getting the opportunity instead of looking for ways to say "no"? Legal needs to educate you and your salespeople and make you aware of the risks without trying to make business decisions, and especially without trying to kill everything with legalese. Of course, every business is different and has unique risks that you need to manage. I'm not advocating skipping a legal review or taking on unnecessary risks just to get a sale; instead, all I'm suggesting is to make sure someone on your legal team is capable of thinking like a businessperson and will find a way to work *with* your sales team rather than *against* them (while managing risks as appropriate). My attorney introduces himself as "an entrepreneur trapped in a lawyer's body," and that's exactly the kind of person who's going to find a way to support your sales team.

Finance and credit also manage risks by making sure that client companies are creditworthy and can pay you, and like legal, they can look for ways to say "no" rather than "yes." If you have a very promising prospect, but a blot on a credit report or some other issue makes them a risk on paper, then you ask, "Can we get creative and find ways to work around that?" Maybe you can't, but the ideal credit department will try rather than eliminate or decline potential business.

A lot of my clients sell heavily engineered products or services, and the technical teams too often say "We can't do this" instead of "How can we do this?" The sales team sometimes needs education on what's possible and what isn't, but both departments share that responsibility. And it's the same with programmers or other technical resources. The mindset has to be "What *can* we do?" The key to getting everyone in the same mindset is communication. Not all communication should go through the CEO, but there must be regular, consistent dialogue among departments, something that doesn't always happen. It's up to the CEO to develop communication frameworks between departments and sales so that everyone can get better insights into how other departments work and sales can understand and think about issues differently, modifying their sales process accordingly if they need to.

GETTING SALES AND OPERATIONS ON THE SAME TEAM

A sure sign of a dysfunctional sales environment is when other departments regularly blame the sales team and the sales team regularly blames everyone else. This was the situation at one of our clients, a software development firm focused on working with mid-market clients to develop custom software to optimize their business systems (ERP, CRM, etc.). A typical project was in the $50,000–$100,000 range and would take two to three months to complete. When Jill, the CEO, called us, she was beyond frustrated. The sales cycle seemed to take forever, projects were regularly underpriced (crushing profit margins), customers were unhappy with the final work product, and her team was in constant turmoil.

We rolled up our sleeves and started gathering data. Starting with the sales team, we asked questions to understand:

- Who they targeted,
- The questions they asked to understand the prospective client's business challenges,
- The questions they asked to help their prospective clients make the business case to invest in custom

software development (generally speaking, they didn't ask many business impact questions),

- How they interacted with the development team to put their estimates together,
- How they presented their proposals and asked for the business, and
- How they followed up with clients once they earned the business and a project was underway.

We then talked to the development team and asked questions to understand:

- When the sales team got them involved,
- Common issues and challenges that caused variances from the project estimate,
- How they interact with the customer,
- Why they are so frustrated with the sales team, and
- Suggestions around how to improve their situation (they didn't have any).

After several interviews, we presented our findings to Jill. To make a long story short, the salespeople viewed the programmers as "the sales prevention department." More specifically, the sales team viewed the programmers as pain-in-the-ass perfectionists who refused to answer even the simplest questions and went out of their way to be difficult. And the programmers viewed the salespeople as bullshit artists who would do or say whatever they needed to say to make a sale. They could never provide the detailed information they needed to give an accurate quote. And when they sold a project, the salespeople would leave them hanging high and dry when the project failed because it was not specified correctly. There was tremendous mistrust between the teams and increasing pressure on Jill to make a change before talented programmers left her company.

The solution? We suggested changing the sales process by creating a low-dollar interim step. Instead of selling the entire project for $50,000 or more, we coached the salespeople to focus on selling a three-hour strategy session to document the client's requirements. They could sell this for $995, position it to the prospective client as a valuable step they could use whether they worked with my client, worked with a competitor, or decided to do the work in-house. And the $995 investment would be applied toward the project if the prospect decided to move forward with our client. This approach created several benefits:

- It created a much shorter sales cycle and allowed the prospective client to become a paying customer at a much lower entry point.
- Nearly every client that invested in the strategy session converted to a full project.
- This basically became a paid sales call—the prospect was now paying for something my client had been doing (very badly) for free before we added this step in the process.
- It forced the salespeople and the programmers to work together to execute these sessions. The salespeople gained a better understanding of why the program-

mers needed more details to provide an accurate quote, and the programmers gained a new appreciation for how the salespeople managed client expectations and asked important business questions.

- And most importantly, the end customer had a much better experience and were more likely to come back when they had a new project.

When you get the sales environment right and get everyone on the same page, great things can happen!

Communication Is Key

As mentioned in the story on the previous few pages, I worked with a software company that had friction between programmers and sales. I talked with the programming team leaders, who said, "The sales team will promise the world, they'll do or say anything to get the deal, and then my guys have to go in and clean up the mess and figure out how to deliver what they sold. Sales has no idea how hard what they're talking about really is."

I talked with the sales manager, and he said, "Those programmers whine about everything. We finally get a deal across the table, and they just hammer us with questions about technical details that aren't really that important."

Obviously, they're not on the same page. They're looking at the same problem but from a different point of view. We reconfigured their sales process by adding a new meeting to define and document the prospective client's technical requirements. Not only did this approach create an incremental sale (for $1,000, we'll help you define and document your requirements), it also helped get everyone on the same page. The customer got a rigorous requirements-gathering process out of it, even if they decided to go with someone else. If they chose to go with my client, the software company, the fee for the meeting would be credited back to them. What came out of that meeting was a crisp document outlining their requirements—basically, the software company's deliverable—and now everyone knew what they were doing.

This was an opportunity for sales, but the real value was getting sales and programming together in a room with the customer. The programmers could see what the salespeople were up against, how they managed the conversation, facilitated the process, and fielded questions. The sales team could see the programmers nerd out with the other technical people and have long conversations about tech things and why those things are important—which to sales was never an important detail, but now they understood. Each side gained a better appreciation for the other side. Adding that one step to their sales process let them convert more sales and raise their conversion rate. The real lesson, though, is how communication between sales and the programmers made the difference and that saying "no" can be a matter of habit.

CEOs need to move the thinking bias toward saying "yes." I think that sometimes departments can slow things down just by being negative and always looking for ways to say "no." So that CEO needs to get above the fray and not be mired in the details, but rather to empower the sales leader to own that type of communication. It's then up to the VP of sales or sales manager to really build relationships and drive the right communication patterns with each department.

What happens when there's a problem and things go wrong? Salespeople find a way to do things that might not be how we want them to do it, but salespeople are often creative thinkers, and they look for ways to do something new. If everyone's mindset is "yes" and "how could we do that?" they certainly need to be able to say, "No, and here's why we can't do it." And then they have to walk it back. People must be empowered to recognize mistakes and address them head-on, and empowering them to do so can be a CEO's greatest strength. People need to be able to recognize a mistake but say, "Let's figure out how we fix it and move forward." Have a rigorous process to review what happened and what you can learn from it. But just as the CEO tells other departments that the company is a sales organization and nothing happens until somebody sells, sales also has to support the other departments by listening and learning. Listen to their guidance if and when they say, "That's not possible, so stop selling it and find a different way."

Your sales team is really your best market feedback loop. They're out there talking to people every single day and finding out what problems are there. And you want them to be creative thinkers, trying to figure out how to solve a problem when they see one. You want them to harness the knowledge and power of everyone in the room or on your team across all these different departments because it's a market opportunity.

I see companies spend a lot of time looking for ways to assign blame. Marketing did this, or engineering did that, or sales did this, and it's just not productive. Ultimately, it's the CEO's job to stop the blame game, and most CEOs are pretty good at setting a culture of accountability and getting rid of the excuse-making in every other department. In the end, everyone learns something. I don't look at situations like these as winning or losing—I look at it as winning or learning.

Questions for Reflection

1. Do you have a process in place to regularly look for potential bottlenecks in your company that could negatively impact sales? And more importantly, do you have a process in place to reduce or eliminate those bottlenecks?

2. Does everyone in your company understand that nothing happens until something is sold and it is everyone's responsibility to support the sales function? Conversely, does everyone in your sales organization recognize and appreciate all the work required to deliver what they sell to your customers? Do they go out of their way to build strong relationships with each department in your company?

3. Do you have a process in place to regularly review sales enablement investments and the return on those investments?

CHAPTER 4

BUILDING STRONGER SALES LEADERS

EACH SALESPERSON ON YOUR TEAM has their own recipe for success, and identifying it is important. But when we work with a company, we spend a lot of time coaching and developing the sales manager, because whatever work we do with the sales team, we need the sales manager to reinforce it every day. A sales manager is a reinforcer and a force multiplier.

Being an effective manager means understanding your team and being in touch with what skills they have and any mindset issues that are holding them back. Managers also need to be aware of some key potential blind spots or mistakes of their own that they might not even know they're making. Sales managers are the linchpin for effectively transforming a sales team; they're your coaches.

Sales Leaders as Coaches

Good coaching for your sales team is the difference between simply pushing hard in a general direction and being specific and targeted in your encouragement. It's also the difference between telling your team to succeed and *helping* them to succeed. Coaching is a big part of a sales manager's role, and it's a crucial part. To be effective, managers must spend more time in coaching conversations than they probably are doing now—if they're coaching at all. Managers who coach more and do so effectively have a massive impact on the team (please see the story in this chapter to gain a better understanding of how much room for growth many sales managers have, and then look at the story in chapter 5 for an example of what can happen when a sales manager follows our system and leverages the data from the sales evaluation).

When our client CEOs introduce us to the sales leaders or managers, every one of them tells us that they spend a significant amount of time coaching. That might be true, but when we peel back the onion a little bit, we find that most of that time isn't productive coaching time. We usually find that they're not coaching as consistently as they believe they are, and the coaching that they're doing tends to be quick hallway conversations, got-a-minute meetings, or ride-along coaching, talking in the car in between sales calls.

That's not ideal coaching, though managers can make use of those situations, and I'll get to that shortly. But first, the foundation of effective coaching is about structure and consistency. We teach clients how to do structured, focused, weekly (or biweekly at a minimum) *required* coaching conversations that are forty-five to sixty minutes long. Coaching sessions follow a format that lets you drill into each salesperson's priorities and current focus, review sales calls that they've completed, and preview upcoming calls. That kind of structured, disciplined coaching focus will make all the difference in terms of transforming your sales organization.

Make Time for Coaching

As a best practice, we tell CEOs that sales leaders and managers should spend 50 percent of their time in coaching and development conversations with their teams. They all push back on this—managers especially—and you should expect that when you introduce structured coaching. Most managers will throw their hands up and tell you that it's just not possible, there's no way to do that. Then you have to look at everything on the manager's plate. Usually your sales managers are spread very thin, but you have to say, "Nope. You *must* free up some time. It's that important." So what about those ride-along calls with salespeople when your managers observe them in the field and the ad hoc got-a-minute meetings? They can work for coaching *if* your manager uses that time the right way.

How much coaching is enough if managers do it weekly? If your manager works a fortyish-hour week, then twenty hours should be spent on coaching, but it depends on how many salespeople are on the team. At a minimum, your manager should spend a couple of hours a week with each salesperson—an hour every week in a structured coaching call (or in-person session when possible) plus an hour checking in with each person. That's a great start and enough to do good, effective coaching.

More pushback is likely. "I have twenty-five salespeople! I can't possibly spend half my time coaching them!" Well, if your manager has twenty-five salespeople, then he or she isn't managing them—they're hanging on for dear life. In this situation, there is no possible way a sales manager stretched this thin can effectively coach each team member to higher levels of performance.

In our experience, an ideal team size for a reasonably complex sales environment is about six to ten salespeople. Once you get beyond even eight, your sales manager may not have enough time to develop and focus on that team effectively. Too large a sales team is a CEO problem—your problem—and I tell CEOs that when planning their sales teams, they can stretch a manager to maybe ten or twelve salespeople, but as soon as they hit twelve, they should hire another manager and split the team in half between the two. And keep multiplying that way as they grow.

What Makes a Good Coach?

What many managers consider coaching is really just a pipeline review, and generally, it's just looking at the bottom of the pipeline. The focus is always on what can close this week, this month, or this quarter, with the sales manager asking where he can be of help. This places a lot of time, energy, and effort on closable opportunities when the manager's coaching goal should be improving each person on the team and thus the team overall.

For each person on the team, managers need to focus on coaching for development versus coaching for production.

For each person on the team, managers need to focus on coaching for development versus coaching for production. Many managers will say, "Hey, this is what you should do. You have this opportunity—do this, do that." For example, if a salesperson is struggling to uncover a prospect's budget, it may be easier and more expeditious for the sales manager to just tell them the questions they need to ask. That may help in the short term with that specific scenario, but the mid-to-long-term impact is that the manager is training salespeople to rely on them when it's time to have a tough budget conversation with a prospect.

They simply direct them and say, "Just do it this way." This always places the focus on the current situation and production instead of helping salespeople work on their strengths and weaknesses, develop new skills, or grow in any way. Instead of giving them the questions to ask to uncover a budget, it's far better to do a role-play exercise to help them practice that conversation or to ask questions about why they didn't feel comfortable exploring the budget at that point in the sales process. This kind of coaching will make a big difference in changing salespeople's mindsets and behaviors. This is coaching for development (focusing on the person) rather than coaching for production (focusing on the problem). While there are times for both coaching styles, long-term success comes when your sales managers invest more time in coaching for development.

The downside to a sales manager focusing on coaching for production is that this can cause big problems with your high-performing salespeople, who will get frustrated with doing things the manager's way because they can't go do it *their* way (and their way is what makes them high performing). Instead, they always have to say "Mother, may I?" to their manager, and they won't want to hang around in that type of environment. So they'll leave, and you'll have more turnover.

Ideally, when your managers spend 50 percent of their time in regular, structured coaching conversations every week with every salesperson, plus the ad hoc conversations that happen naturally, they'll start to see patterns or areas where a salesperson struggles. And that's really what we want because now they know where to *focus* their coaching. They should coach the patterns (the problems, the struggles) and not the situation.

A big breakthrough is often getting the manager to recognize that they'll hear many things in a coaching conversation and might have a hard time picking one or two initial areas of focus. They tend to want to coach everything, and they can't possibly do that. A lack of focus will also keep your team from progressing. We show managers how to find issues and mindsets that become the focus for each salesperson's coaching and plan to work with those issues until they're solved or improved enough to move on to the next issue.

For example, you might find that certain salespeople seem to struggle at the same stage of the sales process every time. Maybe it's when it's time to talk about the decision process, or they're good at asking questions but aren't able to monetize those questions. Say those questions have to do with money, and a salesperson's uncomfortable talking about money. Good coaching would be to give them examples of different ways they can phrase or frame questions to get to a budget or overcome an objection or work through whatever issues they might have covering that topic. The manager can role-play with the salesperson and make the conversation match the reality in the field.

Another area for coaching is mindset issues, which I cover in the next chapter. These are self-limiting beliefs will creep in and prevent salespeople from being as effective as they could be. When managers know what to listen and look for to recognize mindset issues during coaching conversations, and then they can coach accordingly. And when a sales manager can connect this mindset coaching back to a salesperson's personal goals, it becomes even more effective.

Many sales managers, however, never get to the point where they can see the struggles or recognize mindset issues because they're too deal-specific and coach in the moment for production. That's not to say that all coaching for production is bad, because it can be helpful in the short term, especially when it's just more expeditious to tell someone how to do something in a particular situation. That has its time and place, but it shouldn't be the norm. If sales managers make that a habit and that's the entirety of their coaching repertoire, your salespeople will learn to depend on their manager for every thought, action, and direction, and they won't think for themselves. Instead of developing stronger salespeople, you're developing people who depend on their manager for direction, and there's never any progress.

It's best to narrow the focus of coaching to a couple of issues. You'll start making incremental progress and move the needle, and then you can focus on something else next week, next month, or next quarter. When you can do that and coach for development rather than production, your team will start to blossom. As managers get into a rhythm with their coaching, they start to make true progress, and the team's transformation can be remarkable.

Sales Manager Issues

Building stronger sales managers means addressing their mistakes and blind spots too. We see a number of common issues among sales managers that they may not even recognize they're doing.

Playing Favorites

Sales managers tend to play favorites. Maybe one particular salesperson just reminds him of himself or he relates well to another's style.

Some personality types just get along and communicate with each other better than others do. The problem comes when the favoritism shows. Everybody has to submit their expense reports on time, but a few get away with turning it in late. Everyone has to log their calls into the CRM by a certain time, but the manager will let some people slide. Maybe the best leads go to certain people all the time. The team notices these things pretty quickly, and it demotivates them while undermining the manager's credibility.

Sales managers are human, and they can't help but have a favorite player. But everyone should be on equal footing, treated the same, and held up to the same standards. This doesn't mean you manage and coach everyone the same way, but you can't have clear favorites. All team members are expected to attend coaching meetings, do a specified minimum level of activity, turn expense reports in on time, and so on.

The Ted Williams Problem

Baseball player Ted Williams was probably the best hitter of all time. But when he became a baseball manager and a coach, he couldn't explain to people how to hit. He would say, "Well, just look at the ball, and you'll know as soon as it comes out of the pitcher's hand whether it's a fast ball or a curve ball, and then you just hit it. Right? How easy is it?"

We see many strong salespeople who move up to sales manager, and they don't think about how they would teach somebody else the sales skills that made them so successful. They don't wonder, how do I transfer this knowledge? How do I explain all the little things that I do to get this outcome? They've never had to think that way. They're the sales version of Ted Williams: a good salesperson, but a not-so-good manager because they don't know how to pass their skills on to their team—and worse, they don't enjoy being a manager.

As a salesperson, they did it naturally, and what came naturally to them might not come naturally to their team members. Often, the best managers aren't people who were the top salespeople. They were decent salespeople—even good—but they can translate that skill and knowledge to the people on their team. They don't have the "like-me" bias that I see in many sales managers who just assume everyone should do it the way they would do it.

Thinking Your Way Is the Only Way

A friend of mine was a very strong salesperson and built strong relationships with every prospect and customer. He knew everything about them, and that helped him sell more effectively. When he became a manager, he got very frustrated with a salesperson who wasn't like him. That person didn't value those relationships as my friend did. He was still very effective, but he did things differently. It was a blinding flash of the obvious when I pointed this out to my friend and said, "Not everyone's like you, and that's okay. You do it your way, and he can do it his way as long as you get to the same result. If his path is different, do you care, or do we want the sale?" Then he understood that there's more than one way, and he doesn't have to impose his way on his team. To recognize that is an evolutionary step for a manager.

Forgetting What Made You Successful in Sales

Managers sometimes forget what made them successful as salespeople, and often that's their ability to ask great questions. One of the common trends we see for very high-performing salespeople is their ability to just be curious and ask great questions in a way that guides customers and prospects to the answers they want. Yet when these high performers' office doors now say "sales manager" on it, they forget all about how important it is to ask incremental questions, and they start telling their salespeople exactly what to do. They need to translate those questioning skills that they used effectively with prospects in the field and use that same questioning methodology, or Socratic method, to get their salespeople to recognize what they need to do. You can tell a prospect something, and they can argue with you, but if you ask them questions, you can get them to make a statement that's true to them.

You can also apply your questioning skills when coaching your team. If you tell them what to do, they might do it your way or not. They could argue with you or subtly resist. But if you ask them questions and get them to agree to certain outcomes or activity levels, it'll be a lot easier, and it's true to the salesperson. You ask, and the salesperson volunteers what he needs to do.

Trying to Manage People

It's impossible to manage people. So don't even try. We really drill this key concept into the people who go through our sales leadership program. You manage agreements and coach people.

Here's a simple example: Socratically, the manager should ask a salesperson, "What's your goal? How many new calls and new appointments do you need per week to get to x number of proposals to get you to y number of new deals in z time period?" The salesperson can answer each question. Say his goal is $1 million and his average deal size is $100,000, so he needs ten deals—about one a month—and he'll be a little bit over that goal. How many proposals does he need each month to get one $100,000 deal? Let's say two. How many prospects have urgency and you know you're a good fit? Let's say four. How many quality appointments does he need? So you can agree that every month he needs eight or ten net new appointments (about two a week) to keep his funnel full and continue doing that. The salesperson identifies what their activity should be to build up that funnel, and they make an agreement to which the sales manager will hold the salesperson accountable. If the salesperson doesn't reach that goal for whatever reason, then it's the sales manager's job to coach him on what he needs to do differently, maybe discuss changing his approach or give him more resources. Find out what's getting in his way. Is he uncomfortable making cold calls? Now you have a coaching subject. You both agreed to a certain activity level needed to hit his goal, but he didn't hit it, so how can you coach him to make sure that he's able to hit it next time?

MOST SALES MANAGERS ARE TERRIBLE COACHES (AND WE CAN PROVE IT!)

There is an old Woody Allen joke that sums up my view of the current state of sales management in most organizations. Two elderly ladies are leaving a restaurant, and one of them says, "Boy, the food at that place is really terrible." And the other one says, "Yeah, I know. And such small portions!"

Sales managers are terrible coaches, and they do not invest enough time coaching their salespeople to improve sales outcomes. This is not an opinion; this is a fact. For more than thirty years, my mentor, Dave Kurlan, has been measuring sales managers and salespeople across organizations of every shape and size, across every industry, in nearly every country around the world, across every business lifecycle, selling different products and services to different types of buyers at different price points under different competitive pressures—you get the idea. His company, Objective Management Group, Inc. (OMG), has built the most robust data warehouse of attributes that impact sales performance in the world. At the time I am writing this, OMG has gathered data on more than 2.1 million salespeople and sales leaders in more than thirty-five thousand companies (and counting).

What does all this data tell us? It is not pretty. The data suggests that most sales managers do not have the skills required to be an effective coach, do not spend enough time coaching, do not coach consistently, do not coach the right way, do not impact their salespeople's opportunities, do not grow their salespeople, do not inspire their salespeople, do not hold their salespeople accountable, suck at recruiting new salespeople, spend too much time on personal sales and compiling reports, and spend not nearly enough time developing the talent on their teams. It's terrible.

We conducted a data mining analysis of one hundred thousand sales managers evaluated by OMG and found they have an average of 43 percent of the Sales Coaching Competency measured by this evaluation. Only 39 percent of the sales managers in this data set have 50 percent of the Sales Coaching Competency, and a mere 7 percent of sales managers in this analysis have more than 75 percent of the Sales Coaching Competency.

Here is what is measured in OMG's Sales Coaching Competency:

- Consistently Coaches
- Debriefs Efficiently
- Asks Questions
- No Need for Approval from Salespeople
- Controls Emotions
- Has a Sales Process
- Passion for Coaching
- Beliefs Support Coaching
- Uncovers Compelling Reasons to Buy
- Knows How People Buy
- Doesn't Rescue the Salespeople
- Effective at Getting Commitments
- Handles Joint Sales Calls Effectively

For discussion purposes, imagine your sales manager is in the group of 39 percent who have at least 50 percent of the Sales Coaching Competency. Which six areas on this list would you scratch? Which do you believe are not important? How much better would your sales results be if your sales managers were executing in *all* of these with areas? The good news is they can learn how to do all of these and more.

So that is a summary of how bad sales managers are at coaching, but about the portion size? It gets worse. For this, we looked at what salespeople tell us when we evaluate sales organizations. We ask salespeople about the one-on-one coaching they receive from their sales managers and divide the data into these two categories:

1. Frequency of the Coaching Received
2. Type of Coaching Received

Here is what they tell us in terms of frequency:

- Daily   9%
- Weekly   32%
- Monthly   47%
- Quarterly   6%
- Annually   3%
- Never   3%

We recommend a coaching rhythm of at least weekly and sometimes agree that a biweekly schedule can make sense in certain situations (veteran salesperson, longer sales cycle, etc.). And yet, only four in ten salespeople get weekly or daily coaching. With so little coaching, how can a sales manager impact the opportunities a salesperson is pursuing and how can they help them grow and improve? No wonder your salespeople struggle!

Here is what they tell us in terms of the type of coaching received:

- Pricing, Technical, Proposal   60%
- Strategy   6%
- Encouragement, Challenge   12%
- Tactical   7%
- Pipeline/Sales Process   9%

As you can see, most of this is not really coaching. Sixty percent of all coaching is to get technical help or input on pricing or drafting a proposal? That's not coaching. And 12 percent is to challenge or encourage salespeople? That's not coaching, that's motivation. And 6 percent is strategy—maybe you could call that coaching, but I would call that account planning. And 9 percent is pipeline review. I have listened to enough pipeline review calls to know that most of that is discussing "what can we close this week/month/quarter?" and that's not coaching.

The 7 percent of time spent on tactical selling is the only area where this infrequent coaching has the potential to accomplish any meaningful coaching. That is a very small percentage. No wonder 57 percent of salespeople fail to hit quota every year! You read that correctly—more than half of salespeople, across all industries, in different countries, selling different products at different price points, etc., fail to hit quota every year.

To get the sales team you deserve, you must make developing your sales managers your number one priority. When sales managers increase the frequency and improve the effectiveness of their coaching conversations, you will be amazed at the impact they can have—we have seen it time and time again.

Focus Areas to Combat Challenges

No matter who your manager is or how they arrived at that position, there are some overarching elements that should be considered when remaking your sales team. To combat these and other challenges, managers need to focus on the following key areas.

Create a Culture of Accountability

To get the team you truly deserve, you have to raise your standards.

Raise your expectations and decide you'll no longer accept mediocrity. The CEO has to do this first. To get the team you truly deserve, you have to raise your standards. Hire better people, hold the people you have accountable, expect better quality opportunities in the pipeline and higher margin deals being closed, and don't make exceptions.

Connect People's Personal Goals With the Company Goals

One of the best ways a sales manager can raise the bar and hold people accountable is by leading everyone on the team through the personal goals exercise I discussed in chapter 2. True accountability happens when people can see your company as the means through which they can achieve their goals. Everybody wins, and you create an alignment between their goals and the company's.

Set Key Performance Indicators Instead of Managing by Result

Once you understand everyone's personal goals, then you can set some key performance indicators and focus on the activities they need to achieve to reach their goals. I'm not talking about micromanaging by tracking how many calls are made or how many emails are going out. Marking key indicators means being on the same page in terms of a plan and continually checking in on progress. Decide, as a team, what leading indicator you're going to look for, and then work through it each step of the way. Don't focus on revenue goals or *x* amount in sales—that's like coaching a basketball team by only watching the scoreboard. You might know that you're up or down, but you don't know why. You want to look further up the funnel and not just at the result, but say, "To get *x* amount in sales, we need this kind of activity, so let's work through that together, and I'm going to hold you accountable to that."

Cultivate Coaching Skills

Make sure your managers are having coaching conversations that focus on pattern observation and looking at the big picture. Coach for development and not for production, coach to patterns, and don't try to solve everything issue you identify but rather focus on one or two issues. If you have the right kind of coaching conversations and ask the right kind of questions, you should see incremental progress week to week, month to month, and quarter to quarter. For the CEO, you should be able to see that progress in an improved quality of opportunities being pursued, more forecast accuracy, people getting the points in the conversation they didn't before because of their manager's role-playing with them and improving their questioning skills. Cultivating those coaching skills will help overcome the sales manager's issues too.

Motivate and Inspire Everyone on the Team

An important part of the sales manager's job when it comes to motivating and inspiring salespeople is recognizing when they're down and beaten up because they lost a deal. Make sure that they compartmentalize that and leave it behind. They need to be ready to take on their day and not drag into every afternoon meeting with all the rejection they had in the morning. You need to press "reset" for them. No matter how often your salespeople tell you they've put it behind them, you can clearly see that they haven't. Talk with them about the downs and the ups. Tell them they have to let go of the call that didn't go their way that morning and go get the next one. Often, the reason somebody is really crushed by losing deals is that they don't have enough in their pipeline. This is a chance to motivate and inspire, but also to coach. You can say, "So how do we get you to where you're never that dependent on any single opportunity again? Let's focus this next month on not stuffing your pipeline full of opportunities but rather on upping your prospecting activity. How can I help you?" Offer to go on some calls or be an excuse to get appointments with people they couldn't see otherwise—it's amazing how that works.

Recognize that not all people are motivated in the same way. You need to know what motivates each team member and how to use that, and you'll learn things like this when you assess your team, which I cover in the next chapter.

Sales Meetings

Successful sales meetings are difficult to plan and tend to be just status updates for that reason. We've found that sales meetings are greatly underutilized for team development. Managers can make meetings useful, meaningful, interesting, and ruthlessly efficient— whether they're held by phone, an online platform, or in person—if they take time to plan and prepare them around some key topics and the patterns they observe in coaching sessions.

We've found these topics make for interesting meetings, and they encourage full team engagement and participation:

- Best practice sharing. If someone was successful turning a deal, how did they do it? You can ask everyone to plan to tell the team about one best practice that worked for them at every meeting.

- Knowledge transfer. Sales meetings are a great place to share intelligence you might encounter in the field about clients and the overall market. We've seen companies respond to situations that salespeople reported and gain some revenue from it.

- Success stories. Asking salespeople to share success stories can be great if that's how they're motivated. You can role-play what the person did to show everyone what made this sale successful. For those who don't want the spotlight, find ways to make them comfortable sharing the information, like writing a summary before the meeting and just talking about it. On the other side of it, you might be able to encourage some people to share unsuccessful stories as part of their coaching. This is trickier, but you might ask if they mind sharing because you guarantee the same thing has happened to the others in the past. Just be sure that no one puts the person on the spot or embarrasses them.

- Learning. Create a learning environment by having an expert speak about a new product or a thought leader discuss a new philosophy, or have everyone read and discuss a business book.

- Rotate who chairs the meeting. Maybe you've seen a pattern of people not being comfortable with doing presentations.

Put them in charge of the meeting—coming up with the topics, organizing it, and running it. But guide them through this process in one of your coaching sessions to deal with their fear of presentations.

Make your meetings come to life. Don't just have boring pipeline review sessions. Sales meetings should leave everyone feeling a little bit better and inspired, and the sales team should looking forward to them. When you think about the cost of bringing everyone in from the field, it's expensive, so leverage the meetings and get the most out of them. Your sales manager should use sales meetings as an opportunity to elevate the team as a whole so that every month, quarter, and year, you can see consistent incremental improvement. When you start data that helps you understand where everyone can improve (see chapter 5 for more on this) and your sales manager coaches each individual on the team consistently and is able to observe common challenges and opportunities the team is facing to their sales meetings, incremental growth and improvement will follow.

Questions for Reflection

1. What impact are your sales leaders having on your salespeople? Are they investing enough time in coaching, and are they coaching the right things?

2. Have your sales managers created a strong culture of accountability? Does everyone on your sales team understand what they need to do to be successful and the leading indicators they need to hit to reach their goals?

3. What can your sales leaders do to elevate their sales meetings to create more impact?

CHAPTER 5

ASSESSING AND TRANSFORMING YOUR SALES TEAM: CHANGING MINDSETS AND BUILDING STRONGER SKILL SETS

COACHING AND TRAINING alone aren't enough to transform an underperforming sales team. First, you need to understand the full scope of issues and challenges that are holding your team back, and often those are weak or absent skill sets (or competencies) and mindsets that work against a salesperson's best efforts. Addressing both the mindsets and skill sets is absolutely critical to realizing long-lasting, effective change in your sales team. By the way, this is where most sales training fails. There are a lot of sales trainers out there, and many of them are very good, but their programs fail more often than not because they invest most of their time focusing on developing new skill sets. Although these well-intentioned trainers are entertaining and do a great job transferring knowledge and teaching sales tactics and tricks, it doesn't last because their students (your salespeople) struggle to use these tactics in the real world. Why? It's because they don't have the right mindset.

Where do you start? The single most important investment you can make in your sales organization is to benchmark and assess your team so that you can understand the deeper issue and know what kind of help each person needs to improve. To get the sales team you deserve, you need to know where you are so that you have something against which to measure progress.

Assessing Sales Teams

The first step to transforming your sales team is to set a benchmark by assessing your sales team. And you do not need to hire a sales consultant to take this step. You can do it yourself (DIY) by looking at the following:

- Review historical sales data by salesperson, territory, client segment, product segment, or any other filter that is relevant to your business.

- Look for patterns. Which salespeople are consistently high performers? Which sales leaders are driving results across their team? Who are the laggards? Which products or customers are driving more revenue than you expected?

- Review the impact sales leadership is having on the team. How much of their time is invested in coaching? When they are having coaching conversations, are they focused on developing team members (or simply telling them what to do)? Have they created a culture of accountability (or do they tolerate excuse-making—or worse, are they an excuse maker)? How motivated are their team members? Do they understand the different motivational styles of their team members (and that not everyone is motivated the same way or the way the sales manager is motivated)? How is turnover on their team? Do they have enough turnover (or do they enable mediocre performers)? Are they always looking for ways to improve their team, either by coaching each team member or by continuously looking for new sales talent to recruit?

- Evaluate your sales systems. How optimized is your customer relationship management (CRM) solution? Do salespeople have the resources they need in terms of marketing resources (leads, targeted lists, trade show support, case studies), legal resources (prompt contract reviews, attorneys who look for ways to say "yes" instead of "no," etc.), technical resources (access to engineering, technical sales support, a robust demo environment, etc.), financial resources (prompt credit approvals, timely reporting on outstanding invoices, financial modeling for creative pricing strategies, etc.), and coaching systems?

- Evaluate your sales strategy. Does everyone understand which prospects to target and why? Do your salespeople understand how you make money and which products or services drive profit margin? Do they understand how your product or service helps your customers make or save money? Are your sales leaders aligned with the corporate strategy (business strategy, marketing strategy, financial focus, etc.), and are they actively coaching and reinforcing your strategy? When there is a misalignment, how do you find out? Who tells you, and do you find out in time to take action and make adjustments?

All of these areas (and potentially more) should be explored before you embark on a sales development or training program. If you would like to pursue a DIY approach, please visit the resources section on our website (www.intelligentconversations.com/tools) for free worksheets and tools that can help you establish a clear benchmark.

If you decide you want some outside help, there are several ways you can assess your sales team. You can use a one-size-fits-all product that may or may not give you the insights you need, or you can buy a sales training program based on problems you've observed and hope that it fixes everything. CEOs have invested lots of time, energy, and money in sales training programs. Sales trainers, as a group (and I'm in there, right?), are about a dime a dozen. The entry barrier to being a sales trainer isn't that high. You can buy a franchise or read a couple books, and if you're half a step ahead of the crowd, you're considered an expert. Typically, people who are sales trainers are very good on their feet. They're entertaining, engaging, and dynamic, and they can have a modest impact, but often it's not long-lasting. In my opinion, the biggest problem with these programs is that there's a real lack of accountability among many sales trainers—not all, but many.

At Intelligent Conversations, we assess a sales team using our Sales Effectiveness and Improvement Analysis (SEIA). We like this process because it is data driven, yields a ton of data, and is very valuable. We know we can have a dramatic effect on a team, and we can predict how much we can help this person, team, or company improve, and it's a form of accountability. For each individual sales-person, we measure twenty-one core competencies supported by 297 different data points. All of these help us understand that salesperson's potential for growth, where they will struggle and resist, what type of coaching and motivation will be most effective for them, and how long it will take for them to improve, as well as the financial impact for the company if they realize their potential. In other words, we can look at each individual salesperson (and sales leader) and forecast with tremendous accuracy how much they can improve, how long it will take, what it will take, and whether it will be worth the investment. This is all part of our data-driven approach to our program.

We can get such statistics, break them down for a CEO, and say, "This is why this matters." That's when the light bulb goes on and they realize that every sales training program in which they've invested never covered anything like this. They focused only on how to make cold calls or send better emails or learn questioning techniques. All of that's useful and helpful, and, as I mentioned, sales trainers tend to be very entertaining when they deliver it. But if none of that is rein- forced—and especially if it's not also building up a stronger manager

You can't just send your team to a webinar or a seminar and think, "Okay, we solved the training problem."

who'll be there every day to reinforce it and if you're not also working on improving the mindset of your salespeople and their competen- cies—you're going to be less effective. None of it's going to stick. Attempts to fix underproductive sales teams fail because long-term change is hard. We typically engage with a client for six or more quarters—eighteen months at a minimum. We've worked with some clients for years because transformation is a continuous process. You can't just send your team to a webinar or a seminar and think, "Okay, we solved the training problem." You have to build in reinforcement of everything you do. Salespeople will take two steps forward and then backslide into their current habits without reinforcement.

The sales effectiveness and improvement analysis is a diagnostic tool to evaluate your sales team's problems before coming up with a data-based prescription to fix them. We look at the people, the systems, and the strategies that impact revenue growth. We do that analysis to get a baseline of where they are, to recommend our programs, and to measure the impact that we have.

We used to give the assessment results to the sales manager to go through with the team, but we realized the manager isn't exactly our enthusiastic endorser when doing so because the manager might have been burned a little in the assessment. The team thinks it's BS, and the manager would say, "Yeah, you're right. It said I was a bad manager. That can't be right." So it became a self-fulfilling prophesy. We stopped doing that, and now we do the review with the team. I explain that the assessment is one viewpoint on the team. "For me to get a thorough understanding of your skill set and your attributes as a salesperson," I'll say, "I'd need to spend probably three to six months observing you, going on ride-along calls, and coaching you on a regular, consistent basis. That would give me a fuller picture of who you are as a sales professional. This assessment is one lens that we use to evaluate your strengths and weaknesses. We know that it's not 100 percent accurate, but we find it to be *directionally* accurate." It shows us the direction we need to go to work out the team's issues.

We have multiple objectives when assessing a team, but one of the most important is to get a benchmark of where the team is now. We ask specific questions to help us understand your team right now, and that helps us to answer four critical questions for you:

- Can we be more effective? (Every CEO wants to know this.)

- Why aren't our salespeople more effective?

- What will it take to accomplish that?

- How long will it take to accomplish that?

Using the data, we can build a road map for development or transformation and start to work on the issues. The benchmark tells us what's possible and where to focus our efforts. So right out of the gate, what we do isn't a one-size-fits-all approach, but rather it's tailored and customized based on your team. Based on the data, salespeople typically fall into at least three buckets:

- High performers: These salespeople don't have a lot of growth potential, but the incremental growth that *can* be realized can have a high payback because they're selling at a high volume.

- Good performers: Although these people are performing well, they could improve massively with the right coaching and training (if they're coachable, trainable, and are open to coaching and training). With these people, if they're hitting their quota and you're happy with that, understand you're going to have a very low return on training investment and should set your expectations accordingly. The possibility exists that they might not be able to improve much, so think about that.

- Low performers: These salespeople aren't hitting their quota, and they're not trainable or coachable. Now you have to make tough decisions, such as "Should I hang onto these people?" You might need to consider if keeping them is less disruptive than letting them go, which could cause more turnover. You might leave them alone if they're hitting their numbers, even if they aren't going to improve a lot.

Assessing the team with an approach that gives you actionable data lets you examine the team person by person and know who has potential, where the near-term opportunities are for growth, and on what problems and issues you should place your focus.

Here's a small glimpse at some of the data and insights I might get from an assessment: Say we've just assessed a sales team and found that it has two very good salespeople who are crushing it, and everyone else is mediocre to below. The managers aren't very strong, but the team is very coachable—100 percent coachable, which is rare. They're craving help. They're craving coaching, so we either have to coach up the managers to make them stronger or replace the managers and coach the team directly. I won't necessarily know right away which we should do, but you can see that the assessment provided some very keen insights to work with when devising a program.

Now let's look at the two key sets of issues that hold sales teams back: mindsets and skill sets. What's the difference? Mindsets are self-limiting beliefs that creep in and prevent salespeople from being as effective as they could be, even if they've mastered skills. Think of them as fixed attitudes, and they can lead to self-sabotage, even for salespeople with good techniques and tactics. And that leads to skill sets or competencies, which are a set of skills, techniques, and tactics that are particular to a role. Examples in sales are qualifying, closing, relationship building, using social media, CRM savvy, and many more. An example of a tactic is getting the prospect to agree to make a decision on receiving a quote is a tactic. The salesperson might say, "If I could answer all these questions you have and put together a proposal that addresses your concerns, is there any reason you wouldn't move forward?"

Armed with the assessment, we work with salespeople on two levels. Through consistent coaching and implementation, we say, "We're going work on your mindset, and you're going to work on your skill set."

Addressing Core Mindset Issues

If you've invested thousands of dollars and many hours of sales training in the past and later find yourself wondering why it didn't work, the answer is that you didn't address the core mindset issues that hold salespeople back. Learning sales techniques in a classroom setting might yield small, incremental improvement and, if you're lucky, a tiny payback. But to transform your sales organization dramatically, you must work on mindset issues. In the sports world, no matter which sport you follow, there are numerous examples of highly skilled athletes who fail to reach their full potential because they don't have the right mindset. When you have a highly skilled athlete—such as Michael Jordan or Kobe Bryant, who both combined a high skill level with a killer mindset—they are unstoppable. It's the same in sales.

Mindset issues prevent salespeople from moving a sales conversation forward, moving an opportunity to the next step, or asking the tough, timely questions that can stop a prospect in their tracks and think, "Wow, I never thought of it that way before." Assessing your team to find these sometimes hard-to-find self-limiting beliefs is necessary so that your sales managers become aware of them (and the impact they can have on their salespeople) to make their coaching more effective.

In our work, we've observed probably more than a hundred of these self-limiting beliefs in salespeople and sales leaders. We can measure specific self-limiting beliefs empirically when we evaluate a sales team, and these can reveal deep-seated core beliefs that might be getting in the way of a successful sales career. The following are six sales DNA shortcomings that drive a lot of these self-limiting beliefs and can dramatically impact a salesperson's effectiveness:

- Need for approval: This is evident when the salesperson feels it's more important for the client to like them than it is to get their business. This can negatively affect the entire sales process.

- Inability to stay in the moment: Salespeople who can stay present and focused, who can truly listen and just be in the moment, are going to fare far better than salespeople who are easily distracted. Those who lack the ability to stay in the moment tend to overanalyze and start to strategize and think ahead.

- Non-supportive buy cycle: There's a direct correlation between how you buy things in your personal life and how you sell. This is a very controversial marker and is the one that receives the most pushback. Many people are skeptical that the two things are actually related.

- Discomfort discussing money: Salespeople have a hard time bringing money discussions into their sales process. Very smart, capable salespeople struggle with this and lose confidence when it's time to talk money.

- Difficulty recovering from rejection: Rejection is the name of the game in sales, but that doesn't mean it's easy to recover from rejection. Some salespeople are thrown off their game when a deal they expect will close goes south.

- Non-supportive beliefs: This correlates the most to performance. It's a salesperson's collection of beliefs that support rather than sabotage ideal sales outcomes.

There are many small self-sabotaging thought processes—some that tie in to the other DNA markers and some that stand on their own.

Part of our sales leadership program involves helping sales managers to recognize when these DNA issues show up in the sales process and what they should look for. One of the reasons some sales training programs don't work is because they tend to focus on techniques, tactics, and tricks to use on a sales call and don't address these core mindsets. Your team might intellectually understand how to make a cold call, ask questions, discuss budgets, or ask for an order, and they may very well absorb techniques and skill sets they learn in a role-playing workshop or other training. The tactics can sound really dynamic and work well in a role-play scenario in a conference room, but then they blow up in a real-world selling situation. Why? Because if you haven't addressed salespeople's core mindset issues, all of that expensive training will go right out the window the moment they're in front of a client. So you end up making no progress or very limited progress with no lasting effect. This is why it's important to work with a sales trainer or consultant equipped to build a strong sales leader first (see chapter 4) and then work with your sales team and sales leader on improving mindsets.

When a sales manager knows the mindset issues of each person on the team, they really know what to listen and look for when they're debriefing them, and it becomes a framework for coaching to help the salesperson overcome these issues. For example, if I know somebody has high need for approval, one of the Jedi mind tricks we teach is to work with this idea: don't worry about whether or not a prospect likes you—worry about whether they respect you. When you shift the word "like" to "respect," it's amazing how much more confidence you have. Maybe you'll ask better questions and not be as worried about stepping on their toes. Your mindset before you go into the call is now "Win, lose, or draw—I'm going to ask them questions, and they'll respect me by the end of this call. They may or may not like the questions I ask, but they're going to respect me because of it." That one little mind shift can have a big impact.

TRUST THE DATA, FOLLOW THE SYSTEM

I am sure you can imagine the enthusiastic response we get when a sales manager finds out their boss has hired a sales consultant to "help" them transform their sales team. We often spend the first few months of an engagement building rapport with and earning the trust of the sales manager (or managers). Even then, the resistance to our ideas and best practices is palpable. I get it; nobody wants to be told that they are doing something wrong or could somehow do something better. We are always able to work through this awkward transition, and when managers realize we can help them, they begin to implement our best practices. Even then, sales managers often implement maybe 70 percent or 80 percent of what we suggest. Their rationale is they need to tailor our suggestions to fit their sales environment. And generally speaking, we are fine with that approach. In our view, it is better to have a sales manager implement 70 percent or 80 percent, realize significant improvements, and avoid a huge fight to get the final 20 percent or 30 percent of our program implemented.

One of my favorite clients is a parts and equipment distributor that supports various manufacturing processes. Their product set is highly technical, and they sell to engineers, so they like to hire engineers as salespeople. The sales manager is an engineer, and, like many engineers, he looks at the world in absolute terms. Everything is either black or white. When he implements something (whether it is adding a pneumatic control to a food production line or adding weekly sales coaching conversations to every salesperson's calendar), he does it *exactly* as instructed.

He literally followed our instructions word for word and implemented our best practices exactly as instructed. He focused the coaching conversations around the key competencies we measured when we evaluated the team and focused the sales debrief conversations based on each individual and their greatest opportunity for growth. Each conversation produced incremental improvements as salespeople applied the coaching to their sales process.

The results were massive. Veteran salespeople who felt they knew all the significant customers in their territory and had maximized their results suddenly were able to increase revenue by over 50 percent. New salespeople got up to speed more quickly and started having productive sales conversations (and converting opportunities) within six months of being hired (usually it took over a year for a first deal). The inside sales and customer service team started handling transactional orders so the outside sales team could focus on larger opportunities. Average salespeople on the team became good. Good salespeople became great. And top producers found a gear they did not know was there and produced at a new level. Within two years, this distributor went from about $18 million in annual revenue to over $50 million in annual revenue. Sales cycles were shorter, margins were better, and the outside sales team focused on bigger projects while the inside team handled smaller orders and simple transactions. This is what can happen when you leverage data to focus coaching conversations.

Let's look at a couple of these common self-limiting beliefs, and I'll give you a framework for coaching through them.

Belief—Discomfort Talking about Money

This is one of the more common issues that we see. Some salespeople aren't comfortable exploring a prospect's financial situation or asking about what budget they might have to invest in solving a problem. They can be uncomfortable quantifying the impact of the prospect's current challenge that the salesperson could potentially solve. When your sales manager is coaching this person (or anyone on the team), a question to ask is how they uncover the prospect's budget. If the salesperson says, "We didn't talk about budget," you need to find out why they didn't talk about it. One possibility is that the salesperson didn't recognize that they were at that point in the sales process, but the other possibility is that the salesperson was uncomfortable talking about budget and didn't bring it up.

COACHING THROUGH IT

If the salesperson didn't know, it's a relatively straightforward coaching opportunity. But if it's one of these core DNA mindset issues that kept them from bringing up the subject, it's more of a coaching challenge and takes more development. As a coach, you can ask, "What were you feeling when you knew it was time to talk about money and you didn't want to talk about it?" What you'll usually hear is "I started to feel uneasy." In this situation, coach them on how to take a breath, ground themselves, and confidently give the prospect a budget range.

Belief—Having a Negative Perception of Their Profession

This self-limiting belief is more common than you might think. Many negative adjectives can come to mind when some people think about sales. "Pushy" is usually the first word, followed by "aggressive," "slick," even "sleazy." If your salesperson has this self-limiting belief about their own profession, how can they possibly do their job?

COACHING THROUGH IT

We tell salespeople not to think of themselves as salespeople. Instead, reframe their job as helpful problem solvers because having that mindset lets them ask questions that don't push your product or trick the prospect into buying your solution. Instead, the objective of the questions is to learn more about the problem that you can solve. But make sure you really can solve the problem because if you can't, you can still be helpful by pointing them in a different direction. You'll actually earn credibility by directing them elsewhere if you're not a good fit for them.

Belief—Fear of Cold Calls

This is quite prevalent in sales. Despite bloggers and social media experts pronouncing cold calls dead, cold calls are alive and well and will be for a long time. Yet many salespeople are paralyzed with fear when they have to pick up the phone to make cold calls.

COACHING THROUGH IT

Schedule a regular time with the salesperson to make cold calls—at least thirty to sixty minutes blocked out on your calendar, and treat it like an appointment. Change the day and time of these cold calls occasionally so that you might catch someone at just the right time. You can also reframe how they think of rejection, seeing it as a projection instead of rejection. This way, you can start tracking rejections as positive progress toward your goal rather than a negative, and the salesperson can start to look forward to that rejection because it gets them another step closer to a conversation that will go somewhere.

Sales Managers and the DNA Issues

The six core DNA sales issues can also affect a sales manager, but we look at them from a slightly different perspective. For example, need for approval—for a sales manager, we measure both need for approval from customers and from their salespeople. A manager who needs the sales team to like him won't coach them as effectively, ask them tough questions, or hold them accountable as well as someone who doesn't need their approval. Being worried about whether or not they like him will keep him from staying in the moment and being a great listener, so that manager will miss a lot of opportunities to coach them.

What if both the manager and the team have the same issues? If the manager isn't comfortable talking about money and the team isn't either—wow, that company is in trouble. The manager has to help coach the team through that issue, and if the manager herself or himself is struggling with that, the whole team's going to follow.

Skill Sets

Assessing skill sets tells you the weak spots in your team's abilities. We measure twenty-one of these core competencies for both salespeople and sales managers (they differ slightly, but there's a lot of overlap). This baseline assessment of each team member's skill sets helps us design our program and identify development priorities. Here are the ten selling skill competencies we measure:

- Hunter: the capabilities for prospecting, how well they hunt for new business

- Reaching decision-makers: a salesperson's ability to reach people who have the authority to buy

- Relationship building: the quality of a salesperson's business relationships

- Consultative selling: the ability to take a consultative approach to a sales opportunity and uncover the compelling reasons to buy

- Selling value: the ability to quantify the opportunity and be the value rather than sell on price

- Qualifying: the ability to thoroughly qualify an opportunity

- Presentation approach and context: the ability to present the right content to the right people at the appropriate point in time

- Closing: the ability to get business closed on a timely basis

- Milestone-centric sales process: the ability to follow a staged, milestone-centric sales process

- Embracing sales technology: the mastery and discipline to use sales enablement tools, including CRM, social selling, and selling remotely over video

Most sales training programs you might invest in typically begin and end by focusing on improving selling skills, and in many cases, the content is delivered in a highly generic way. We recommend an approach that is more tailored because every company faces a different sales environment. First, start with a solid sales methodology that provides a proven framework while offering tremendous flexibility to customize to any situation. Then build a milestone-centric sales process designed for *your* sales environment. Again, this is where many generic sales training programs get it wrong. They take a one-size-fits-all approach, and they don't care if you're selling commercial roofing, commercial insurance, or a software-as-a-service product—it's all the same to them.

You can have the sales team you deserve by starting with mindsets and:

- Assigning different learning tracks to each salesperson based on their findings, and then

- Teaching sales leaders how to recognize and coach salespeople to reinforce the transition to a stronger sales mindset, and then

- Introducing a customer-specific, milestone-centric sales process calibrated for your specific sales environment, and then

- Teaching selling skills in the context of that sales process with real-world examples from your sales environment.

These skill sets are all important, but the last five can be important depending on what you sell—for example, social selling. Some of my clients are very active on LinkedIn, and it works for them, so this skill is important for them. Real estate agents are another example of people who really need to be active on Facebook. But many of our clients are in industrial sales, and social media platforms aren't where their customers go to do research for those types of products. Presenting is another important but not highly important skill to watch, even though it might apply no matter what you sell. Most salespeople are really good at presenting; almost everyone is solid at that.

Sales managers should focus on the first five in the list. These five skills are the ones that sales managers should really watch in each team member. Let's break down a skill set. Hunting, for example—someone who's low in this skill needs help figuring out how to prospect better, how to work past the gatekeeper, and how to make better cold calls. Another is closing. There are ten different attributes to being an effective closer, and about half of them relate to skills. We find the weak areas to address in coaching.

However, for sales managers, we look at sales *management* competencies instead of selling competencies, and a few of them are the same competencies I just mentioned. Relationship building, for example, is important for a manager both in terms of building relationships with your customers and your team. But management competencies include their ability to coach, hold people accountable, motivate, and recruit.

Post-Call Debriefs

I mentioned how sales managers can use post-call debriefs to spot evidence of mindset issues on their team. These debriefs are also a quality control and inspection point. When the manager knows that someone has a need for approval, another person can't control their emotions or has difficulty in certain situations, and the manager knows what to listen for or look for when debriefing a sales call, imagine how much more effective the sales coaching can be. Salespeople can slide back into old habits very quickly. With this inspection point, a manager can make sure that they're applying the training, doing it the right way, and not slipping back into their habits.

Transforming a sales team starts with assessing these competencies and mindset issues. But even if you succeed at a transformation, you should still be recruiting salespeople—not just when you need them, but constantly. The next chapter covers building a recruiting program that will keep you from making hiring mistakes.

Questions for Reflection

1. Can your sales team be more effective?

2. How much more effective can they be?

3. What is it going to take to achieve that?

4. How long will it take?

CHAPTER 6

HIRING SALESPEOPLE

THE SHORTEST PATH to getting the sales team you deserve is to upgrade your mediocre salespeople by hiring better salespeople. And yet nearly every CEO and business owner we work with is reluctant to do so. Nobody likes to fire people, and most CEOs and managers will do anything to try to avoid it. If your team is underperforming, you might consider investing time in upgrading salespeople through coaching and programs such as those that Intelligent Conversations conducts. It's an option, but it's not always the right option depending on an individual's coachability and willingness to be coached, not to mention the time and disruption involved. At the same time, you're probably not anxious to recruit and hire new people for a host of reasons (mainly because you might not have a solid sales hiring system in place, and it's easier to just stick with the team you have). But doing nothing about a weak performer does more harm than you may realize. It actually weakens leadership, shows indecisiveness, and makes the high performers on your team wonder why they're working so hard and question whether they want to continue to work for you.

Fire or Upgrade?

Taking the time needed to upgrade an underperformer is a big decision, but don't keep someone on the team for the wrong reasons. If they can't sell, they can't sell. I think sales managers sometimes overestimate their ability to coach low-performing salespeople and get them back on track. Instead of holding them accountable, managers look at their pipelines through a hopeful lens and think that closing this deal or that deal will get them back on track. Remember the accountability discussion about managing agreements and coaching people. Performance targets are an agreement that sales managers must define and manage. So set an annual sales goal for individuals, divide it by twelve (or whatever's appropriate if your business is seasonal), and hold them accountable for doing at least that much. If they fall behind, then the manager has to redouble efforts to get them back on track. Understand, though, that you can't let that go on and on forever.

When we engage a client, we start with data. We measure everybody on the team, and from that, we get a good sense of whether or not they'll be coachable and how much friction implementing change could cause. If we don't feel that someone will be open to coaching, we don't immediately recommend firing that person. We give everybody a chance and put them in our program, but along with that, we start implementing our sales hiring system so the client can build a pipeline of potential replacement candidates while still giving that person a chance to improve. But you still need to set expectations and say to underperformers, "Everybody's on this plan, including you, and we're going to talk again in thirty, sixty, or ninety days." The salesperson might not realize it, but they're on a short runway while we're implementing other systems to help build up a bench of potential candidates to replace them.

Hiring brings CEOs and managers a different set of headaches, mostly because they don't have good hiring systems in place, especially when they really need quality candidates immediately. Often there's a disconnect between sales and human resources that makes hiring quality salespeople difficult, so sales leaders once again hang on to middling or low performers. I talk with many sales managers and VPs who don't have a very high opinion of HR. Managers don't want to work with HR because they believe that HR doesn't understand what they need, which only frustrates them. Personally, I think this pain and suffering is perceived and not real, but most sales leaders would rather keep the underperformers and hopefully coach them up instead of dealing with HR through a long hiring process.

From the human resources team's viewpoint, the sales leaders and managers are nonresponsive and don't give HR the information they need. They believe that sales leaders reject too many of the candidates HR presents to them, often without providing any feedback or direction on why. HR feels they're continually guessing. Because of this disconnect, much of our work when implementing our sales hiring system is in getting human resources and sales on the same page and speaking the same language.

Having a solid recruiting system in place makes it easier to hold a sales team accountable to the agreements the manager sets, and if they don't or can't live up to those, it's honestly better to free them up. Often, when word gets out that leadership finally fired an underperformer, the other team members validate it with

It's not fun to fire people, but having high standards and holding salespeople to their agreed performance targets are crucial to building a culture of accountability.

comments like "Finally!" or "It's about time!" Then they rally and are thankful that the company let the person go. Even customers can validate the decision to fire, saying, "I'm glad you let that person go." Either way, you might learn things you didn't know before and wish you had paid attention to much earlier.

It's not fun to fire people, but having high standards and holding salespeople to their agreed performance targets are crucial to building a culture of accountability. To be clear, it's equally important to give underperformers every opportunity to succeed and to provide coaching and support to help them get back on track. You can have high standards *and* be empathetic in the process. Set a timeline, communicate with the struggling team member, and provide support, and if they can't succeed in their current sales role, either find a new position for them or let them go. Building a good recruitment system can make it easier to let underperformers go when you reach that point.

Building a Recruitment System

Finding quality sales candidates takes time—anywhere from two to four months, and even longer in a fully employed economy. The time frame can also depend on how much industry knowledge and technical expertise a salesperson needs. The recruiting time frame might increase beyond two to four months if your sales are more technical or you need a strong salesperson with highly specialized skills or knowledge.

We recommend that sales leaders always have their line in the water, and it's why we recommend and implement our Sales Talent Acquisition Routine (STAR) hiring system. Remember, a decision to recruit is not a decision to hire. This system helps you maintain a passive search so you can always be recruiting at a low level. Even if your team is at full strength and all of your territories are covered, I still recommend keeping a job ad out there or putting a position on your website and being open to hiring opportunities as they come in. You might find someone who's very strong, and then you have decisions to make, such as how to integrate the person into the team, who you would need to let go, and whether or not you could create a new position for this person.

Good salespeople are hard to find—great salespeople are more uncommon and difficult to find. So when one comes into your network or process, you should be ready to make a decision. I think most sales managers and many sales teams and companies run reactively rather than proactively. They recruit only when they absolutely have to, usually after they've kept someone for too long and it's blatantly obvious that the person has to go. Then they start flat-footed and have to build up a pipeline quickly. They end up compromising and settling for the best available candidate instead of having good candidates waiting in the wings from consistent, low-level recruiting. We call that a virtual bench.

Create a Virtual Bench

Intelligent Conversations teaches companies how to recruit salespeople and create a workable recruiting program that builds a virtual bench of quality candidates. A virtual bench has many benefits:

- You're in a good hiring position when you need someone immediately and won't have to take what you can get or settle for mediocrity.

- Salespeople are more accountable and motivated if they know they're replaceable, and often the overall caliber of the team improves.

- Your company becomes more attractive to candidates and to your existing salespeople (a subtle motivation because high performers want to be around other high performers). When you bring someone in who's equal to or even better than your current high performers are, it forces everyone to have a culture of continuous improvement and pushes everybody to be better than they are.

A virtual bench strategy requires you to be well networked and in contact with the top salespeople in your industry, even if they work for a competitor or an adjacent industry. The best salespeople in your industry or adjacent industries are working somewhere already and might not be looking for a position. If the sales manager keeps tabs on these high performers (seeing them at a trade show or having lunch or dinner now and then, for example), they can call that person when an opening is available. Don't worry—it's not weird to suddenly call someone with an opportunity and ask if they'd want to even consider it if you've already had several conversations with them. There's nothing awkward about it.

You can even network with your customers. Ask them if there's a salesperson they really like and respect who is looking for opportunities or works at another company. You'll be surprised how many good leads you get from them. If a salesperson could win the business of your well-liked and respected customers—even if they don't sell your exact product or service—chances are they can transfer into your space.

If the economy is good (particularly in a fully employed economy), another option is to use a recruiter. As painful as it can be to pay anywhere from $25,000 to $40,000 to a recruiter, you'll be much better off to pay for a recruiter's talent if you have a critical position to fill and need high-quality candidates quickly. Recruiters can be worth every penny in those circumstances.

Define Position Requirements

Defining position requirements is crucial and must focus on the realities of the position. Intelligent Conversations uses a comprehensive profile to help determine sales position requirements and set the bar that candidates have to clear. In most companies, determining requirements is often the source of disconnects between HR and sales. HR might give the sales manager a position profile or a form to fill out, but the form doesn't always address the realities of the position. Salespeople work in a different environment than people in other departments do. They face more rejection, and they sometimes face hostile situations in which prospects lie to them or competition says bad things about them. It can be difficult to convey these situations using an HR form. So it's extremely important for sales managers to be crystal clear about a position's realities and requirements and have a lens through which to look at it. Think about your best salespeople. Why were they successful before coming to your company? What skills would transfer? What things are unique to what and to whom you sell?

For example, if you sell to C-level people—chief technology officers, chief information officers, chief marketing officers, and the like—your candidate must be capable of having that level of conversation. You can't accept a junior candidate who doesn't have that experience. You could hire into a junior position and train them up, but not if you need more experience right away. So be specific about the requirements—This is a senior sales position. The candidate must be capable of selling in the executive suite, they must have done it before, and they must be able to tell stories about how they did that successfully. Similarly, if you need a certain level of technical knowledge, define that. Your candidates must show success in navigating *your* kind of environment, as well as selling for companies of a similar size as yours. Also, consider the sales cycle, the sales size, how many presentations they're making, and to whom they present (one decision-maker or a group of decision-makers in one or more meetings). We use factors like these to create a comprehensive profile that helps us set the bar for candidates at the correct level. Then we use that to calibrate our preemployment assessment to help us understand what a candidate has done successfully and if they meet all of the requirements.

Effective Hiring Interviews

Salespeople can sell, which means they can handle interviews better than non-salespeople do, so you need a rigorous interview process to get past their ability to sell you on themselves and see the real picture. Intelligent Conversations focuses strongly on interviewing techniques and strategies as a key to successful recruiting because the truth is that most companies aren't very good at interviewing and don't know how to do it effectively. You need a list of topics that you'll cover in every interview—not necessarily an exact script or set of questions, but you should explore the same areas in every interview within a structure. That said, interviews have to be a bit free-flowing and not too rigid.

Managers can be reactive and often just show up to an interview and wing it if they don't have time to prepare for it. That's problematic for any position in your company, but it's deadly when you're interviewing salespeople because of their interviewing skills. Typically, they can out-interview even the strongest HR person and most anyone else. They just can. They're used to being in that situation every day when selling, so they tend to be bright and articulate, and they can read the room, read the response you're looking for, feed off your body language, and react by adjusting what they say based on how they read you. To get past that ability, you need a very different interviewing system, one that puts salespeople to the test.

In the next sections, I'll describe how we interview candidates in our STAR hiring system. It's probably different from any method of conducting interviews you've ever tried. We focus on interviewing techniques and strategies used within a structure. I'll mention here that good candidates actually like being interviewed in this way. One client who's using our STAR system sent me a recording of an interview and asked what I thought of the candidate. When the interview was finished, the salesperson said, "This has been a good interview. You really challenged me, and I appreciate that. It isn't what I expected, and I hope I answered your questions, but it was refreshing to be challenged." To me, that's a sign of a good salesperson, when they can acknowledge a challenge and appreciate it.

PHONE INTERVIEWS

We recommend interviewing every single sales candidate by phone first, whether or not your salespeople sell by phone or face-to-face. The phone is still a key tool for any salesperson, yet most companies don't conduct phone interviews with sales candidates, and I don't know how else you can learn how someone will perform on the phone except to have them perform on the phone for you. We recommend highly structured (though not scripted) and outlined interviews, starting with a very rigorous six-to-eight-minute phone interview that's direct and to the point.

Be forewarned that these challenge interviews will make your human resources team uncomfortable. It is important that you help your human resources team understand that hiring salespeople is different and the cost of a hiring mistake is even greater when hiring salespeople. Our interviews put sales candidates under pressure to see how they perform. A rigorous interview that simulates an actual sales call will tell you a lot more about a sales candidate than a polite resume review. Our interviews are not rude or unprofessional, but they're definitely all business and very much to the point. We change topics quickly and often challenge the candidate on the spot. It takes some practice and confidence to conduct this type of interview, but it is worth it because the sales candidates who can get through will be strong additions to your team.

Here is an example of how we do it. Let's say I ask about a candidate's prospecting activity and how many cold calls they make, and they say fifty calls a day. So I'll challenge that. "Great, let's do some role-play. Let me hear your call. Ring, ring! Hello, this is Mike." If somebody makes fifty cold calls a day, they'll go right into it, but if they are exaggerating how many calls they really make, they'll struggle under the pressure I just placed on them. Next, I read some of the key job requirements and ask them to tell me how they meet those requirements. I'll follow up on what they say and probe a bit. After that, I hit prospecting and pipeline development, territory development topics, what a busy week looks like for that person, and more. Then I quickly and abruptly ask them to tell me about how they close—how they know it's time to close and what words they use.

Then, just when the candidate gets comfortable with the pace, I pull the rug out from underneath them. "Okay, listen, I'm running late for my next call. If you hear from my assistant by four o'clock tomorrow, you're moving on in the process, and that next interview will be a video interview. If you don't hear from my assistant by four o'clock tomorrow, that means this is as far as you go."

It's a jolt, right? I stop and don't say another word. I'm looking for that salesperson who asks a follow-up question or asks for feedback, such as, "How did I do compared with others you interviewed today?" But frankly, I don't care if they ask me what size hat I wear. I want to know if they can handle a put-off and if they'll ask a follow-up question. Most candidates will meekly say, "Okay, thank you," and then hang up. I want the person who has the backbone to push back a little and ask for feedback or what the next step is in the process, maybe tells me a joke to break the ice and create some laughter. I can conduct this interview in about eight minutes and cover a lot of ground while finding those intangible qualities that are hard to pick up and hard to coach if they don't have them. Plus, I experience their phone presence and personality. It's very important to do this phone screening before meeting the candidate in person so that you form a first impression based on their phone presence, particularly for business development reps, who are typically younger kids right out of college and whose entire job is to book appointments by phone for outside salespeople. If the candidate passes the phone interview, they move on to the next interview.

IN-PERSON OR REMOTE VIDEO INTERVIEWS

Effective in-person interviews with salespeople aren't like typical interviews that human resources departments conduct. Like the phone challenge, in-person interviews are also challenging and need to reflect a salesperson's daily environment with pressure similar to what they face in the field.

We often conduct these interviews by video because our clients are all over the country, and by doing so, we found some valuable, unanticipated benefits from seeing their ability to organize themselves for a web interview. Do they understand technology? Can they get their webcam set up correctly and connect to it? Do they still put on a suit, even though the interview is remote? What's in the background? (Is the cat walking on the kitchen counter behind them?) How's their camera presence? The answers to these questions are important because selling today often involves remote demos and presentations. Paying attention to these factors really paid off in 2020 because our clients' salespeople needed to sell remotely.

Like the phone interview, the in-person or web interview is highly structured and direct. Again, I'm not acting rude or unprofessional, but I'm definitely not warm and friendly either. I put pressure on them. A typical interview lasts forty to forty-five minutes. I go through the candidate's résumé—their career transitions, career path progression (is it logical, and if not, why not), and the successes they claim. It's amazing to look at the bullet points that salespeople put on their résumés. "At this position, I grew sales by 75 percent." I ask them to clarify that. "Tell me what sales were when you got there and then when you left, and how did you get to this number?" Often, they can't do the math and don't have the story behind that claim. They just randomly put things like this on résumés.

I continue challenging the claims they make, asking why they left their job. If they were let go, I might say, "Usually, high-performing salespeople aren't let go. Tell me why they decided to fire you." You wouldn't ask that question in polite conversation or at a cocktail party, but the purpose of these interviews is to simulate the pressures of the sales environment. Candidates will face adversity on sales calls, particularly when calling on prospective customers who might not be very interested in talking to them. Prospects will be direct and even rude, and candidates will have to navigate through that. These interviews are a trial run of how they'll perform in the face of adversity.

You can pick up a lot of other information about the candidate from being direct in this way, and it's a better, more efficient use of your time. I like to record both phone and video interviews (with the candidate's permission) because we can add them to the candidate's file, and anyone involved in the next round of interviews can review these recordings and know what's been covered.

FINAL INTERVIEWS

Candidates who get through the phone and video interview move on to another interview with others in the company—for example, the hiring manager and maybe a sales support person or someone from marketing. We might conduct an entire series of interviews, especially for a position like sales director. Orchestrating the interview sequence and determining who will cover which topic keeps the different managers from asking the candidate the same questions. Interviewers from different areas of the company should ask questions that make sense for them to ask.

Any candidate who passes all of these interviews comes in again for another interview, but now I turn the tables a bit. I'm no longer in a challenge mode. I still interview and qualify the candidate because I might still need to gather more information, but my main goal now is to inspect cultural fit to see how they'll blend in with the team. I want a broad range of perspectives on that, so I involve several additional people. The interview this time won't be as structured as the others were. Maybe we'll all go out and eat a pizza together. But in this situation, everyone talks about who they are, what they do, what territory they cover, and their individual role. They ask some questions, but it's really a chance for the team to have input and involvement, and the candidate can meet the team and learn about them.

At the end of the day, the CEO interviews the person, and this time it's all about selling them on the opportunity. Great salespeople like to be sold. They want to see if you qualify them and if *you're* asking the right questions. For example, if the position requires a move, ask, "Did you talk with your spouse about the possibility of moving cross-country for this position?" or "Will this be disruptive for your kids?" Talk about your company's growth path and how hiring them would get you there faster. These things get candidates excited about the position and the opportunity. For younger candidates, you might have a career-mapping discussion and tell them what others who were in the position went on to do within the company. For candidates at a mature career point, emphasize stability and the company's strengths. For all candidates, be able to describe what you do and why it's significant in a way that motivates, inspires, and attracts high performers. Try to connect whatever it is you do to something bigger. For example, a packaging company could say, "We're a packaging company." Reframing it, they could say, "We ship products made in this country" or "We get products to market safely" and show people the broader impact they can have if they work for you. It's highly attractive to people when you can describe what you do in a way that recognizes the value you create beyond the transaction.

Salespeople want to work for the money they can make, but more important, they want to be part of something larger than themselves.

Salespeople want to work for the money they can make, but more important, they want to be part of something larger than themselves. A strong, purpose-driven corporate culture and environment mean something, particularly to high performers. They want to work for a company that has mojo and momentum. Make them like the experience they're seeing.

SALES HIRING SUCCESS

When CEOs and sales leaders follow our STAR hiring process and begin to see the immediate jump in talent they can bring on, they often wonder why they put up with mediocre salespeople for so long. Hiring salespeople is difficult. It is probably the most difficult hire to make because as I have said, even a mediocre salesperson can out-interview a strong HR manager or even a strong sales manager who only interviews occasionally. There are a lot of client stories I could share on this topic, but the one that comes to mind is a SaaS software company in the fintech market space. When we first started working with the CEO, Joe, his sales team had seven outside salespeople and three inside salespeople with a different sales manager for each group and both managers reporting to Joe. They had annual revenue of about $30 million.

After our initial analysis of the sales team, we predicted that at least half of the salespeople and one of the sales managers were unlikely to improve. However, we always recommend giving everyone a chance, so we started our coaching and development program while also telling Joe that we needed to start the STAR hiring process immediately because we wanted to build a strong pipeline. As predicted and as often happens, a few of the salespeople and one of the sales managers started resisting the changes we were suggesting, made excuses, and did not want to be held accountable. Fortunately, they had built up a strong candidate pool, and we were helping them interview outside sales candidates. Within six months of starting our program, Joe added three new salespeople who better matched their sales environment and were able to get off to a strong start. He did not need to fire anyone; two of the excuse-making outside salespeople as well as the always-complaining sales manager decided on their own that they should go somewhere else.

While our coaching and development program lasted about eighteen months, I continue to keep in touch with Joe, and his firm continues to use our STAR hiring system. Of the initial twelve salespeople we evaluated when they were a $30 million company (ten salespeople and two managers), only four remain. Their annual revenue is now over $50 million, and they have better profit margins, shorter sales cycles, greater client engagement, and a stronger sales team that is hyper-focused on serving their core customer. When you raise your expectations and follow a proven system, you, too, can see this kind of growth.

Compensation Strategy

One of the most difficult conversations we have with CEOs is about setting compensation for sales positions because CEOs often think big on requirements but low on compensation. This doesn't reflect the reality of the market for a quality candidate who meets incredibly high standards.

Sometimes it seems like CEOs want somebody who has an advanced degree, thirty years of experience, and is under age twenty. That's a joke, of course, but they can come up with ridiculous requirements sometimes that compensation-wise would be a million-dollar salesperson. "No, I'm going to pay them $60,000." The compensation has to be in line with the position's requirements and difficulty. But they'll argue that $60,000 is what they've always paid salespeople. "Why would I change what I've always paid salespeople?" is *not* a strategy for successful hiring. If a sales team is underperforming and I show the CEO what "good" looks like and the investment that's required to get that, they have a hard time accepting it. But a high-performing salesperson will run circles around three mediocre salespeople, and they're worth every penny. You get what you pay for. If you're willing to fill your shop floor with top-of-the-line machinery, then don't be surprised when the B-level salespeople on your team can't perform at a high level. You have to invest in all areas of your business.

There are many ways to structure compensation in sales, and it should always be done with the market in mind. Some teams have straight commissions, others have commissions that kick in after they hit a certain threshold, and some companies prefer a base salary with a bonus based on performance—the salesperson's, the company's, the team's, some combination of those, or all three. You can pay commission based on revenue or on gross profit, depending on how much control you want the salesperson to have. If they are paid on gross profit (rather than top-line revenue) their interests will be aligned with the company as they negotiate on price. But if they do not have that authority, then it is often easier to simply pay on revenue.

I believe you need to pay salespeople a base salary and am generally not a fan of a commission-only sales compensation structure. I don't want salespeople worrying about whether they can pay their rent or mortgage next month, but I also want the base salary to be small enough that they're not quite comfortable and will have the drive and motivation to earn variable pay. If you overpay on base salary, your salespeople might not have much get-up-and-go. They're perfectly happy with their base, and anything above that is gravy. Salespeople always have to be a bit hungry.

When discussing compensation with new hires, I like to talk about what they'll make in their second year. Why? The first year is a ramp-up period (learning the company and market and building a pipeline). The pipeline should be full by month twelve, and then they make money in year two. This is what they can realistically expect. Then on-target earnings for year two have to be based on realistic targets (if it's a variable pay plan, which we recommend). The sales manager has to be able to explain how all of this works in terms of what they're selling, the sales cycle length, average commission, how long it takes to build a pipeline, and so on. This shows them exactly what their path to compensation looks like. I'm a fan of uncapped commissions, so if the salesperson really crushes it, they should make a lot of money. In fact, I want salespeople to be the highest paid employees in the company. I want the best of them to make more than the CEO does. Some business owners and CEOs get upset when I say that, but when you think about it, if you've structured their compensation right and they're making more money than you are, that means your company's growing and you're increasing your company's value. For owners and CEOs, it means fatter distributions at some point as the sales team continues to have success. Ultimately, it's up to the owner to build enterprise value and keep the company growing, and you have to pay for that.

Making changes to the comp plan is the number one reason why salespeople leave their jobs. CEOs often change it when they see how much salespeople earn (and particularly if it's more than the CEO earns). Nothing's more frustrating to a salesperson than when the company moves the goal every time they feel like they've figured it all out. Just set the comp plan and leave it alone. Take the time needed to structure the comp plan the right way and make sure that it incents the right behaviors and then let it stand. Modifications are necessary sometimes, but make sure that any changes are a win-win for everyone—the salesperson, the company, the owner, and the CEO.

A Quality Business Problem?

Suppose your hiring system works so well that you find salespeople who are better than your top salesperson? This is a quality business problem, the kind of "problem" every business would like to have. What do you do then? Consider the constraints:

- Can you fund the position?

- Do you have resources to train and develop someone new? Will that disrupt the manager's schedule? (Most sales managers underestimate the time needed to spend with a new hire.)

- How would adding this person affect production capacity? If you already have constraints in your manufacturing or your ability to deliver, a wildly successful high performer will make things much worse—worse than not bringing him onboard at all—and damage your reputation in the marketplace.

Create a Solid Onboarding Plan

Finding great candidates and hiring them can all go down the drain if you don't have a good onboarding plan in place to help them succeed. The lack of a good onboarding plan is often a company's biggest hiring mistake because a new hire's first ninety days are crucial. You can't go through all the time, energy, and effort to recruit and then bring them on board and expect them to figure everything out on their own.

You need a good, structured onboarding process and need to be very deliberate about its elements. For example, specify in your plan who will:

- Show new hires where to find all company resources

- Explain a typical sales call

- Role-play and practice with new hires

- Introduce them to other departments, especially who to call for technical help

- Explain when and how to bring other departments into the sales process

- Provide a basic understanding of all products and services and how you price those

- Take them on sales calls to observe how you do things

- Watch them when they do their first calls

These are just a few broad items to include in an onboarding plan. In our work, we like to include what I call a voice-of-the-customer exercise sometime in the first few months of onboarding. I believe that selling is about telling stories, and good salespeople are good storytellers. A new salesperson doesn't have stories yet. Sometimes high-performing salespeople find ways to make stories from their past jobs relevant to their current situation until they develop their own stories. In this exercise, the new hire gets information to start creating stories. Your sales manager identifies six to ten customers (ideally happy or mostly happy customers), calls the customers, and explains that a new salesperson is going to call to ask some questions. If you have good relationships with your clients, it shouldn't be hard to find some who will agree to do this. I like the new hire to ask a set of three questions:

- Why did you choose to work with us? (What problem did we help you solve? Why did you choose us versus anyone else?)

- Is there anything we could do better? (Where could we improve?)

- How would you build a portfolio of business or find customers if you were in my position? I'm new to this industry and company.

Asking such questions lets the new hire hear what amounts to a firsthand review of your company's strong and weak points but from a friendly, helpful voice. For example, the customer might say they chose your company because of your support team, your outstanding quality, your distribution centers, and the way those centers cover their territory. When asking what you could do better, the new hire will hear some negative things—"You're great for the most part, but sometimes your shipping is late, or your invoice doesn't match your actual work." They might even uncover problems that they can take to the manager or appropriate department, and that gives you the chance to address those problems. For the third question, customers tend to give generic advice that the new hire might already know, but it's possible to get a gold nugget that's actionable. "Hey, I know exactly who you should call. In fact, let me introduce you." That's gold when that happens.

The new hire writes down everything the customer says because these answers are the foundation of the stories they can tell when they go out on their own sales calls. When a prospect asks why he should do business with your company, the new hire can give examples of why customers choose your company over others. You might even have him do a presentation in a sales meeting, which will benefit even the veterans on your team.

For accountability, you should stage out what new hires should know within a set time. This gives you a time frame and an agreement. For example:

- Within thirty days: have a basic understanding of products, services, and pricing

- Within sixty days: completed the voice-of-the-customer exercise; be ready to accompany and observe a senior salesperson on calls

- Within sixty to ninety days: be ready to go on calls with the manager or other senior salesperson so they can observe you

- After ninety days: book own appointments, go on calls alone, know where to find resources and whom to call for technical help, and so on

Generally, you'll know within the first thirty to ninety days whether a salesperson's going to make it or not. Often, you know in the first thirty days but might give them the full ninety days to ramp it up. If new hires can't adhere to your structured onboarding process, be prepared to pull the plug. Recognize your mistake (you made a bad hire) and learn from it rather than hang on and hope that things will get better.

The transformation frameworks laid out in these chapters should yield improvements in your team. If you consistently upgrade the talent on your sales team with each new hire and then coach and develop your new salespeople as they learn your business, you will begin to see a dramatic change in your sales performance. In the next chapter, I discuss the results and ways to measure your success.

Questions for Reflection

1. How many salespeople would you hire if you knew nine out of ten would be successful?

2. How strong is your onboarding plan for new salespeople?

3. What is the typical timeframe between hiring a new salesperson and revenue?

CHAPTER 7

THE RESULTS: WHAT THE TEAM SHOULD LOOK LIKE

STEPHEN COVEY TAUGHT US to begin with the end in mind, so to get the sales team you deserve, let's invest some time in defining exactly what the sales team you deserve should look like. At the start of your transformation planning, it's important to think about what success looks like for your company because you need something against which to measure your efforts. Most CEOs want to measure success by revenue, and though it's a sign of a winning sales team, increased revenue is just one part of the successful picture. Obviously, revenue growth is important and we all watch it, but as I discussed, revenue is a lagging indicator, so you won't see your success

Revenue is a lagging indicator, so you won't see your success as quickly by watching revenue alone as you will by looking at other signs of improvement.

as quickly by watching revenue alone as you will by looking at other signs of improvement. I think a lot of companies have an anything-for-a-buck mindset, but they start to realize that not all revenue is created equal. Firing some of your lower-paying clients and focusing on higher-paying clients that really drive revenue and margin and fit what you do exceptionally well—that's part of winning.

Winning means different things to different companies, but you should see some common indicators of success.

Signs of Success

Look for leading indicators. For example, how many new appointments are your salespeople making every week or month? If they're having the right kinds of conversations with prospects, you should be seeing more and better appointments from everyone on the team. Are you seeing higher-margin sales? You should be able to sell projects or products at a higher margin at this point because of strategies such as letting go of certain customers who, even though they might have been with you from the very beginnings of your company, are low-margin customers and don't fit your new model. What kind of movement do you have from one stage to the next in the pipeline? Are you seeing shorter sales cycles and pipelines that are more active? Is everyone performing to the high producer?

I want to discuss two big signs of success that will feed your growth. The first is that you'll attract better quality candidates for sales positions. Once you're seeing the results of your improvements, be assured that others in your industry will see them, too, especially high-performing sales talent looking for new opportunities. They might even come knocking at your door because now you have the sales team that everyone wants to join. It's almost as if you're the envy of everyone in your industry, even your competitors. When the best salespeople see what's happening at your company and start losing sales to your company, guess what they want to do? They want to jump ship wherever they are and want to know "How do I get in there?" Believe me, salespeople will walk up to you at conferences and trade shows and ask how they can apply for a position. So your efforts can certainly pay off from a recruiting and retention perspective. And again, this raises the bar for the entire sales team, and your newfound popularity will be very obvious to your low performers. The low performers on your team might even opt out on their own because they won't like being with your company anymore (the spotlight of accountability is too bright). They liked it when they could turn in their sales reports once a quarter and nobody bothered them. Now, they have to talk with their manager every week and discuss what they're planning for the next week, and they don't like that. They'd rather just fly under the radar.

The second is gaining a growing clarity around your core customer. It might sound crazy (and it's a very big shift in mindset), but when you're operating the right way, have sales leaders who really manage people and hold them accountable, and your salespeople are having the right kinds of conversations with the right prospects, you start to get better customers. This is when you might suddenly have the luxury to pick and choose projects or turn away customers that don't fit your model. When a sales team is struggling, they'll accept whatever sale they can get—it's the anything-for-a-buck mentality at play. Part of that is because CEOs tend to focus on just ringing the bell to get revenue. In this way, CEOs are sometimes their own worst enemy because they create an environment that tells salespeople to just get sales, to just get quotes out. That puts pressure on the sales team, and they just start doing anything they can.

When your sales organization is successful and hitting it on all cylinders, they can be a little more discerning about who they allow into your customer portfolio. You're in a position where you can accurately predict the revenue you need, and now you gain that clarity around your ideal customer—the right kind of customer for you, the kind you serve better than anyone else can. That's a very narrow slice of the market, but they'll drive almost all of your revenue and profit. You can be hyper-focused on those that you align with best or that really need, appreciate, and value the product or service you offer. Opportunistically, if revenue falls into your lap and it's convenient, sure, take it. But always put your proactive focus on the ideal customer. Let the rest of your competitors slug it out over the rest of the market that's lower margin, a bigger pain to sell, and is harder to serve. And it doesn't end there. Even after you have great customers, you'll continue to refine that and get even better customers.

Downsides of Success

Success has a downside. Just when everything is going smoothly, things can happen within your team that can set you back and, if not addressed, can wipe out all the hard work you did to transform the team.

Managers Fall out of Rhythm

Sometimes managers go on autopilot when their team starts running smoothly and think that if everything you've done to get to this point is working, then you're good. This is why it can be helpful to work with an outside resource who can spot this before it becomes a problem and serve as a catalyst for additional development. We have clients who ask us to check in at least once per year to make sure they do not lose momentum.

How can you spot this before it becomes an issue? Spot-check your sales manager's calendar and take note when they fall out of their regular coaching rhythm. Maybe they have started skipping a week here and there and have eased up a bit on accountability. Keep an eye on the team sales meetings because it's amazing how quickly it can regress to a tactical pipeline review again instead of a proactive development meeting. It takes time to get back into the meeting rhythm if no one holds the manager accountable. This is when things can slip very quickly. As a CEO, you need to push your managers continually to focus on the next thing you can improve.

The team has a rhythm, too, and sometimes, they're thrown off their rhythm just because life happens. I had a client who was highly compliant with our program, but one time, the sales manager got the flu, and then half of his team got it too. He was embarrassed when he told me that they just fell out of their rhythm when they all got sick. My advice was to get back on track as quickly as possible. Business happens, too, and busy salespeople will miss a meeting now and then. They're going to trade shows or are tied up responding to a big RFP that demands all hands on deck. But if you start seeing people skipping meetings across the board for no good reason, step in, find out what's going on, and remind everyone that those meetings are part of what's making you successful. Salespeople and sales managers often don't want to admit that simple things like regular well-structured meetings are actually what's making them successful. Ego gets in the way. They think it's all about them and how brilliant and incredible they are. They're crushing their numbers, so they feel they don't have to meet every week. If you let that continue, you're no longer looking ahead and will have to make more dramatic, severe course corrections. Sometimes they just lose sight of the importance of maintaining a consistent meeting rhythm and the one-on-one coaching sessions. You can't rationalize it to yourself because you still talk with everyone on the team and do some coaching here and there. It's not the kind of focused, disciplined, and structured coaching that made you successful.

Whether business or life gets in the way, you should anticipate a certain amount of disruption at times and be ready to deal with it. Sometimes the signs of a loss of rhythm can be nearly imperceptible, but you'll see them if you're alert. It's important to get everyone back on track as quickly as possible.

A Lag before Results from the Initial Implementation

Just as a lag occurs before you see results from the initial implementation, there can be a lag when the team and manager's rhythm falls off, which means you won't see the impact right away, but it's still happening. When we work for a client, we usually spend six months overhauling their sales infrastructure. Then we spend another six months implementing a new selling system and teaching new habits, mindsets, and skill sets. After that, it can take six months of reinforcement to maintain the new habits, sometimes three to six quarters of activity. Then add on the sales cycle. All told, it could be twelve to fifteen months into the program before the results start to show. You have to continue reinforcing and maintaining the work, even after a program like ours ends. A CEO once told me, "Mike, the true mark of your impact will be measured by our ability to execute the program without you watching us." He was right. Our goal is to transfer knowledge and give sales teams the tools, methodologies, habits, and behaviors to continue to succeed long after we're gone.

Many struggle with sustaining the process without us and have to correct the course further down the road. It's up to the managers and the CEO to keep it going and make sure everyone remembers what made you all successful so that no one drops back into old habits, even when you think you've solved the issues.

Success can breed complacency when success becomes the new normal.

Temptation to Backslide into Old Habits

Success can breed complacency when success becomes the new normal. It's easy for your team to start resting on their laurels, and this is one of your biggest risks at this point in the transformation. It's easy for them to start taking wins for granted and maybe not work as hard or ask as many questions. Backsliding can happen very quickly if you don't watch for it, so keep a keen eye out for any signs of complacency.

You need to constantly remind your salespeople and managers about their new habits any time you see even a hint of old habits returning, Personally, I'm always learning and growing by going to learning events and getting coaching. And yet, there were times when I was among a group of peers who are some of the top sales trainers in the world, and someone reminded me of something that I used to do consistently. I had just stopped doing it, and I don't know why. Maybe I got busy or distracted, but I fell out of the habit. Always being in a learning and growth environment reminds me of the positive behaviors and habits I used to do. Vigilance and continuous reinforcement are necessary to prevent backsliding.

CONSTANT CARE AND MAINTENANCE

A few years ago, I was enjoying a pint of beer in Vancouver, British Columbia, with my good friend and colleague Brad Giles from Perth, Australia. Not only is Brad a successful business coach and author, but he also asks great questions and provides keen insights. This is one of the many reasons I asked Brad to review an early draft of this manuscript, and I promise this is a much better book after incorporating his feedback. As we were catching up, he asked excellent questions about my sales coaching practice and shared a powerful analogy.

He said the work I do with B2B sales organizations is really like building a beautiful garden. Maybe it was the pint(s) of beer, but it took me a moment to fully appreciate his point. And as usual, he's right.

Building a beautiful garden (and building the sales team you deserve) takes constant care and maintenance.

- You need to consider the environment (competitive context, business lifecycle, ideal client, etc.).
- You need to select the right plants (Are you hiring salespeople who can thrive in your environment? Are the sales managers you have hired spending enough time coaching the team?).
- You need to control weeds (excuse-making, complacency, discounting, poor follow-up, lack of systems, etc.).
- You need to group plants around a theme (campaigns, market blitzes, product/service focus, cross-sale promotions, etc.).

- You need to incorporate a little whimsy (testing new approaches, encouraging creativity, taking risks, adding fun competitions to keep everyone on their toes, etc.).
- You need clear borders and boundaries (market and territory planning, account assignments, lead workflow, etc.).
- You need to feed the soil with rich nutrients, and you need to let it rest periodically (training, coaching and development, off-site meetings, etc.)
- You need to focus on long-term results—are you building a garden (or sales team) that will thrive for generations?

Too often, CEOs and sales leaders look at training and development as a transaction. It is something they know they need to do, so they look for the easy answer so they can check it off their list. If you truly want the sales team you deserve, approach it like you would if you were building and maintaining a beautiful garden. Take the long view and give it your constant care and attention. Thank you, Brad. I love that analogy.

The New Challenges of Success

Success brings a new set of challenges. How do you keep growing? How do you make sure that the program you've implemented stays strong and continues to work for you? Most important, how do you keep salespeople engaged in the transformation and always pushing themselves to improve? Here's how to address those challenges.

Maintain Your Momentum

Don't take your foot off the gas—you must maintain your momentum. Business owners and CEOs need to keep pressure on sales leaders to focus constantly on what got you to where you are. It's human nature to drop the level of discipline required to maintain the sales team you deserve, so be sure your sales managers do not fall into that trap. Continue executing the things that are making you successful, like running better sales meetings, conducting more effective, disciplined, and structured coaching sessions, and spending at least 50 percent of their time coaching. All of those things are making them successful. Remember that part of this journey of transformation is deciding to be the best and then deciding to *stay* the best by always improving. And it's never over, really. Being the best and staying the best is always a work in progress, and even if you think you're done, there's always another level and something more you can do. You have to push that limit continually so that you're getting better every month, every quarter, and every year. You can look back and say, "Look at all the progress we made from when we first started, and then every year we keep getting better." Be vigilant and maintain good habits, and be ready to recreate positive behaviors if they fall by the wayside. That's the ideal state.

Watch Your Competition

As your success leads to more dominance in your market segment and you get the cream of the market (that 7 to 10 percent of the market that's the most profitable), you need to be alert and watch your competition because they covet those customers too. You might find new competition, too, because your clients could get on the radar of a larger national competitor that starts to go after your customers aggressively. Be prepared to counterpunch when competitors approach those customers with discounts or incentives to try to steal that business. Know what you're going to do next. Circle the wagons around those core customers and say, "We're seeing some of our customers getting some irrational pricing from our competition, so you're probably going to get that too. Just keep in mind that the low price often brings the greatest risk. I'd hate to see you make a short-term decision that's going to impact you in the long term." If you built the right kind of relationship with these customers, led them through the right kinds of conversations, and are serving them well, you shouldn't have any concerns about losing them.

Prepare to Invest More

As you grow and continue to succeed, you might suddenly find yourself dealing with a strong competitor you've never had to face before. You might be invited to bid on larger opportunities that you've never been in the running for until now. These are more of those quality business problems, but you have to be ready for them. These will be welcome because you're continually pushing and striving for that next level. Many of the clients implementing our program find themselves in such situations and have to make additional investments because of their sales success. It's a great measure of what you can expect once you have the sales team you deserve. Don't be caught thinking, "Hold on, I have too many clients. I don't know what I should do right now. My factory's operating at capacity. I have to add a big extension." Problems like this make you the envy of your marketplace and aren't a bad thing if you're ready for them.

Work with Data

Always check your data. Make sure that you're maintaining margins, that your critical ratios through your sales funnel are maintained, and that there's diversity in opportunities in the sales pipeline. Diversity and opportunities could mean making sure that you're not too concentrated in one segment or one industry sector. It could also mean deal size diversity if all you're doing is hunting for very big deals—and that's great when you get them. But make sure you have medium and small deals, too, because those will help maintain a steady growth rate.

I can't say this enough: make sure that you're measuring your sales team and new people as they come in. Use the same standards that you used to evaluate your team to make sure that you hire only the best and bring in people who are as good or better than your current salespeople are.

Raise Your Expectations

Now is when you can stop settling for mediocre and stop compromising. You decided to be the best, and you held everyone to that decision, but now you really have to hold yourself to it and keep on raising your expectations. Stretch your team and push them each quarter, every year, because at this point, things that they would've thought were impossible a year or two before your transformation suddenly become very possible. But you have to keep pushing them and raising expectations—both yours and theirs. Never let your team get into a mindset that they're only good enough to sell at this price or that margin, and don't let yourself believe that you're only good enough to hire a middling or low-performing salesperson. Accountability is key in so much of the transformation process. You must hold everyone accountable to continue improving, especially yourself. Accountability can be hard. Sometimes the nicest sales manager in the world isn't doing what you ask him to do, so he has to go somewhere else. Sometimes that low-margin customer has to go. Those are hard conversations to have. I've fired clients before, even if I like them or they had been with me for a while. But they were taking too much of my time for the revenue they gave me. Even though letting them go was necessary, it was still hard to do.

Look for the Next Thing

Now that you're seeing what a high-functioning sales team can look like and the quality of your problems improves, you don't want to go back to where you used to be. Now you need to think about what's next because it's not over, not by a longshot. What else can you do? How can you be even more hyper-focused? How can you be even more selective about the customers you pursue? How can you charge even more for a product or service? The fact that it's never over is one of the things that I love most about what I do. There's always something else to keep improving and reaching for that next level. You can always find a way to be a leader in your market, industry segment, and community. When you do that and have a success mindset, everyone will be attracted to it, and you'll find yourself continually upgrading your team.

Challenges Elsewhere in the Company

Let's look outward at the rest of the organization and see how what you do in sales could affect them and create challenges. Sometimes a sales team's great success creates pressure in other parts of the business.

I've had clients tell me that they had to pause our program because they had an operations issue or couldn't keep up with the quotes or had to hire more engineers. Everybody and every department in the company must be ready for the possibility of the sales team being a little successful—or even wildly successful—because it can certainly be a challenge.

Your success can quickly expose any weaknesses and glitches in your system. Think of a leaky garden hose. You can turn up the water volume and suddenly see holes in the hose, and the more you turn up the water, the worse those holes will get. If all you're looking at is what's coming out of the end of the hose, you won't see the leaks even if a ton of water is coming out of them. So if you don't have enough engineering capacity or quoting capacity to keep up with your now high-functioning sales team, be prepared to invest in those functions because the quoters or engineers you have will be quickly overwhelmed. A successful sales team can create operational pressure or customer service issues because operations can't keep up with the sales team's momentum. This certainly affects your clients. If you're scaling too fast or selling too fast and you run into operational problems, the longer lead times and maybe a perceived drop in service (or a real drop in service) will frustrate your clients. You must be able to execute and manage that growth. I've seen companies grow, grow, grow, and then they struggle because they can't keep up and their operations fail.

You need solid communication among all company managers to avoid such issues. For example, the VP of sales should communicate with operations as large orders make progress through the sales pipeline and coordinate closely with accounting and finance to make sure invoices are accurate. Also be alert for any signs that other departments are resting on their laurels. With so much new money coming in, it's easy to allow for a little operational inefficiency and maybe not be as stressed about billing promptly because money's rolling in. You must be vigilant about maintaining discipline across all of your systems as sales increases. Make sure you're communicating proactively and investing in those areas too.

These are more CEO "next thing" issues, but the framework is a bit different because it involves solving problems created by your sales success instead of looking for the next thing to keep growing. Your sales team is firing on all cylinders, and you have to keep that going. Ask yourself, "Where is that creating problems? What's the next thing I can focus on?" You might have to work on operations, marketing, finance, or customer service. Now that you've built an efficient sales engine, is that creating a customer onboarding issue? Is it creating a throughput, operations, or customer retention issue? You have to keep an eye on that while making sure that your customers are happy and your non-sales employees aren't killing themselves because they're under stress. I think the fact that there's always something else that demands your focus is really the fun part about business because it's a continual evolution. Just keep an eye on it and make sure that you're staying ahead of the issues.

Consistency is the key to addressing all of these new challenges—always trying to get a little bit better, making incremental progress, and consistently applying the strategies and tactics that got you to where you are. You're reaping the benefits, but you have to keep raising the bar and challenging your team. Reinforce the winning mindset. You're good, you know you're good, and you're going to keep getting better. Think about why people are doing business with you, even though you're more expensive now and more selective about your customers.

When to Throttle Back

Increased sales can cause you to rethink the team you have on the field, and not just from a sales perspective. Do you have the operational capacity to handle your growth? Do you have the finance capacity? Do you have all the other pieces that you need? Sales doesn't operate in a vacuum. It affects everything else in your organization. Is it possible to grow too much? There can be a point of diminishing returns, and you could hit your limit. You might need to sit at this level for a while.

If you see the wheels starting to come off as you scale, maybe you have to throttle back a bit. Just get used to this. Usually, an operational execution issue is the warning sign. Sometimes it's a capacity issue—you have only so many machines that can make only so many widgets, so all machines are fully operational six days a week for three shifts. You look at that throughput and might have to decide to run at that level for a while before making a capital investment. So run at that level, be profitable, and build up your balance sheet so you can make that next big investment if you see that you're growing too fast. You don't want to end up in trouble. Too many sales coming in too fast is definitely a quality problem—but not really because if you can't deliver, it's no longer a quality problem but a *big* problem. You have to decide when you can no longer sustain growth. At that point, you still work the strategies that got you to where you are so you can stay successful.

Questions for Reflection

1. What would your company look like if you followed this road map to get the sales team you deserve?

2. What would you do differently if your sales organization were performing at the same level as your other departments?

3. Now that you have read this far, what are you going to do to take a step toward improving your sales function? What can you do right now to take action?

CHAPTER 8

TAKING ACTION

Sales Team You Deserve—Checklist

Check off which of the descriptions below applies to your business and consult the corresponding chapter for help where you identify areas of weakness or opportunities for growth.

1. CEO FOCUS AND COMMITMENT

❑ CEO understands how their previous experience impacts how they interact with the sales organization, has a plan to improve, and is actively working to improve and optimize their relationship with the sales organization.

❑ CEO is willing to do whatever it takes—including letting go of or reassigning loyal, lower-performing salespeople— to get the sales team they deserve.

❑ CEO is committed to hiring and coaching a strong sales leader to drive revenue growth and professional growth for every salesperson.

2. CLEAR GOALS—BUSINESS AND PERSONAL

❑ Sales leader (or CEO if there is no sales leader) has clearly identified the ideal clients to target and has communicated that to every salesperson.

❑ Sales leader (or CEO) has identified the key milestones, pipeline metrics (number of appointments, number of discovery meetings, qualified proposals, etc.), and sales activities to reach the company's sales goals.

❑ Sales leader (or CEO) has met with each individual salesperson on their team to understand their personal goals and to help them align those goals with sales activities and company goals. In other words, each salesperson can see the company as the means by which they can achieve their personal goals.

3. SALES ENVIRONMENT

❑ The company regularly invests in and consistently optimizes sales enablement technology (list sources, CRM platforms, lead generation, etc.) to support sales.

❑ We have identified clear sales messaging, and both sales and marketing are aligned around how to engage our ideal clients and lead them through a conversation that helps them see how we might (or might not) be able to help them.

❑ Sales leader (or CEO) has good relationships with every other department, and the other department leaders are sales focused and openly collaborate with the sales leader to support revenue growth.

4. BUILDING STRONGER SALES LEADERS

❑ Someone other than the CEO or owner is responsible for driving revenue growth, coaching and developing salespeople, managing the sales pipeline and forecast, managing the sales environment, setting sales strategies, etc.

❑ Sales leader (or CEO) holds regularly scheduled, consistent, and structured coaching sessions with each salesperson focused on coaching for development.

❑ Sales leader (or CEO) holds consistent, productive sales meetings that keep everyone in the sales organization focused, aligned, and motivated to drive growth.

5. ASSESSING AND TRANSFORMING YOUR SALES ORGANIZATION

❑ The company has completed a benchmark study of its entire sales organization and knows the sales team can be more effective, how much more effective, what it will take to realize that potential growth, and how long it will take.

❑ Each team member is working with their manager or an outside coach to follow a customized development plan that will help them improve their selling skills as well as their sales mindset.

❑ Progress is regularly monitored and measured so the development plan can be modified based on the team member's progress (or lack of progress).

6. HIRING SALESPEOPLE

❏ The company has clearly defined each sales position, knows the skill sets and experienced required, and conducts regular reviews to ensure compensation is relevant to the market.

❏ Sales leaders and human resources work together to maintain a constant search, whether or not there is an open position, and can move quickly if a strong candidate becomes available.

❏ Sales leaders and key managers who interact with sales have strong interviewing skills and know how to manage the conversation with a strong salesperson.

7. RESULTS: WHAT YOUR TEAM SHOULD LOOK LIKE

❏ Our sales organization has clearly defined goals and metrics that are regularly reviewed by our sales leaders and are consistently achieved.

❏ We have our pick of the best clients and best projects in our market and are able to sell our product or service at a higher margin than our competitors.

❏ We can count on our sales forecast to be accurate both in terms of timing, revenue, and likelihood of success. Our leadership can make plans and investment decisions based on the accuracy of our sales forecast.

8. TAKING ACTION

☐ Based on the answers above, I feel I have the sales team I deserve.

☐ Based on the answers above, I can clearly see where we need help and want to manage this transformation by myself.

☐ Based on the answers above, I can clearly see where we need help, and I want to get some help to manage this transformation.

How We Can Help

CEOs and sales leaders often know what they need to do to transform their sales teams, or at least have some sense of what needs improved. It's like dieting. Everybody knows what needs to be done. You're trying to lose five pounds, so you log all of the food you eat to make sure you're eating the right foods in the right amounts, but not everyone does it consistently, right? You know you should eat specific things and exercise more—you got that, you've been told that your entire life. And yet if your kids are sitting around eating potato chips and pretzels, guess what you'll end up doing? It takes consistency and discipline, and it's the same thing when trying to transform an underperforming sales team. The change you want doesn't happen overnight but comes from consistent, good decisions—small decisions—built up over time. It's about deciding to have a world-class sales team. It's about raising expectations and then holding the sales leadership team and the sales team accountable to raising the team's expectations.

But not everyone can implement a sales team transformation in a disciplined, focused way. That's where we can help. Intelligent Conversations offers a methodology to ensure consistent application of simple concepts and principles, commitment to following through on them, and changing mindsets across the sales team—building new behaviors and habits and reinforcing them consistently. These three things are the only things that will really change a sales organization. You can get there on your own, but you'll get there faster if you work with professionals like us.

I often say that what we teach isn't new, and it's rare that we share something that's revolutionary. A lot of our work in transforming sales teams is based on common sense, and often the teams and sales leaders we work with find many of the concepts are familiar to them. Plenty of sales trainers and authors have paved the way and written extensively about the concepts involved in transforming sales teams. But what really changes a sales organization is doing a few small things with greater consistency and discipline: sales managers focus on coaching for development versus coaching for production, salespeople listen to customers and prospects better and ask better questions, and they become more comfortable talking about money and working on their self-limiting beliefs, for example.

Yes, you can probably make changes on your own. This book gives you a framework to start doing that. We believe we can get you there faster and with great impact, not because we're better than you are, but because we've seen a lot more than you have. To get the best results and the sales team you deserve, you will need:

- Data from our Sales Effectiveness & Improvement Analysis (SEIA) to make the right decisions,

- Accountability and structure from an external party,

- Experience from our previous engagements and the plans we have executed with hundreds of companies, and

- Ownership over the results from an external party.

This is our specialty. We've been down this path before and know the traps and pitfalls, how to navigate through the change process, and how to implement it all with discipline and focus. Plus, we're an outside party who can hold you accountable. You'll make some improvement doing it on your own. But if you work with someone like Intelligent Conversations—and this is what we do all day, every day—you'll probably get there faster, mostly because of the accountability element.

Our Services

I was on a call once with a company's chief learning officer. She asked, "Can you just send me a list of all your services?" I said, "Well, I can, but Intelligent Conversations doesn't have standard services. So I need some more information to know what's relevant to you." I explained that everything we do is highly customized to an organization depending on the data we gather about the team, individual salespeople, and sales leaders. But that said, typically there are some common themes.

Our programs start out with the team evaluation because it's the single best investment you can make if you want real transformation. You have to know what you're working *with* before you know what to work *on*. I'm always amazed when companies invest obscene amounts of money in sales training programs without knowing if it will even address their issues. I'll ask, "How did the training company come to recommend what they're doing for you? How do you know that the training you're buying is what your team needs?" The answer I often hear is "Well, that's the training they offer. That's just their program, and we bought it." All I can say at that point is "I'm sure their content is very good." Anyone in the sales training business has good stage presence and can be entertaining, and they have good content. Tell me how they measure the return on investment (ROI) for their program. They may have a small impact for a little while, but it won't be a sustained impact, and that's where the hard work begins, just when many sales trainers get their check, cash it, and get out of there.

Intelligent Conversations isn't in the seminar business by choice, and I've turned down keynote speaking opportunities because I know it's not going to make a difference. I can go and whip up a sales team with the best of them, but that's a one-and-done thing that doesn't make a lasting impact. To do that, you need somebody to guide you through a tailored, customized program that's based on several things that are specific to you: what your team needs, your selling environment, your place in the market, the competitive pressures that you face, your product set, the average sale price or ticket price of your product or service, the length of your sales cycle, and your customers. You need a clearly articulated strategy, and then you need to understand who on your sales team is capable of executing that strategy. All of that leads into our process, which is about as close to a services list as I can get considering that everything we do is customized.

EVALUATION

Our programs begin with a thorough evaluation of the sales team because it is the single best investment you can make if you want real transformation. Every engagement with Intelligent Conversations starts with a detailed analysis of your existing sales organization. It's typically a month-long project; we do a deep dive to help us understand the strengths and weaknesses of your team, inspect your systems and processes, and inspect your sales leadership team to determine if your team will get better, how much they can improve, what it will take to get there, and how long it will take. We look at a whole range of issues and present that data to the CEO.

DATA INTERPRETATION

The quality and accuracy of the data we gather in this process is powerful. We can review 286 different data points for each team member and hundreds more when we look at the entire team. We have been running these evaluations for more than fifteen years and have evaluated well over two million salespeople—and over that entire timeframe we have continually refined and updated their findings to reflect changes in the sales environment. For example, when COVID hit in 2020, we added a competency for "Video Selling," as salespeople needed to change how they engaged the marketplace in the COVID economy.

So when we review the data with a CEO, we often hear comments like "Oh, that's it, you've nailed it. That's our team" or "I've never thought of it that way, but what you're saying makes sense. Now I understand." These are light-bulb moments for the CEO, and those reactions tell us that our data is accurate. We know that it works. It's not perfect, and there might be a little noise in the data here and there because it depends somewhat on the sales team's full engagement and participation. The opportunities are there for some directionally accurate (but not perfect) information that we can interpret and tell the CEO, "Here's where you need to focus. These are your near-term opportunities for growth."

ROAD MAPPING AND PLANNING

We literally use a whiteboard to start drawing out a road map, quarter by quarter, to start improving the sales organization. Based on that road map, we come up with an estimate of the investment required that depends partly on how fast the CEO wants to change. We always look for a quick win—something that can have an immediate impact and build momentum. That said, some of the changes we recommend could take several quarters to take hold. It really depends on how committed the CEO is to change and the pace of change the organization can handle. If a CEO wants to transform faster, it might take more of our time up front, and we'll do that.

BENCHMARKING

The evaluation identifies the issues that need our focus. It also provides a meaningful benchmark of the team's state and status, which gives our program a starting point and something to measure against as the program progresses. You wouldn't go on a diet without first stepping on the scale to capture your starting point. Many sales trainers don't want to anyone to measure their performance. I tell CEOs right up front, "Hold me accountable. This is how you hold me accountable. We're going to measure it now. If I'm any good at my job, we're going to measure your team ten months from now, and you should see improvement. If you don't, that's on me." We always see improvement.

FOCUS AREAS

One of our big focus areas is sales infrastructure, and that's typically in the first quarter, sometimes up to two quarters. This includes sales leadership development, mapping out your sales process (which most companies haven't documented and haven't really thought through as a very detailed, milestone-centric process), and, often, working on sales messaging (which can become a sales playbook) and implementing a selling system. Infrastructure is the foundation for change, and no one would make much progress in other areas without that foundation in place. Most sales trainers don't spend the time building the infrastructure, and it's so important because it's a reinforcing mechanism for after our program that gives the managers everything they need to keep it going.

In tandem with that, we work with the salespeople individually to help them understand their mindset issues and give them tools and exercises to work on those issues on their own with their managers coaching and reinforcing the improvements. Within three to six months, we make tremendous progress, though it's not yet visible because it hasn't translated into revenue dollars. But the salespeople will have stronger mindsets if they do the work we ask them to do. The sales managers at this point are having better coaching conversations if they do the work. The sales infrastructure is in place, including a milestone-based sales process and consistent sales messaging. We've mapped out the ideal target accounts and the logical entry points to those accounts. All of this happens by six months. Then we start to implement a training program.

TRAINING AND DEVELOPMENT

We implement a two or three quarter sales training program that could be a combination of online learning, webinars, workshops, and seminars. I prefer live training, though it's not always practical to do that logistically. Sometimes I can plug training into existing in-person meetings. In between training, we're in regular conversations with sales leaders, doing webinars, or doing group coaching calls with the sales team, and we're also in touch with the CEO to report on what we're seeing. We want to make sure that the CEO is becoming the CEO they need to be to lead a high performance sales organization and to help them navigate through any problems.

After a couple quarters of sales team development, implementing a selling system, and developing the right kind of skill sets, we continue to work on mindsets. At that point, we're twelve to fifteen months in. Now the transformation is well on its way, and you can look at it objectively and see clearly that the team is having better conversations, higher-quality opportunities entering the sales pipeline, and regular, consistent, stronger coaching conversations focused on development, not productivity. This is when they start to realize revenue, depending on the sales cycle length and how quickly the team implements the training. By the end of four or five quarters, we can dial back the frequency of how much time we spend with the team, and now we go into reinforcement mode. How long we stay in that mode and the frequency required to support their continued growth is different for each client. Usually, we're in this mode for at least a few quarters, although we've had clients keep us on for reinforcement for years because they have experienced the impact we have on their sales team and they can easily measure a return on their investment. We will recommend a sales team maintenance program for clients to consider that will help their sales team remain at their peak so all the good work we have implemented together will have a lasting impact.

COACHING NEW HIRES

It can be awkward when a new sales hire comes in midway through our program or after our program's over, so we developed a set of online tools that a new hire can use to get up to speed on our selling system quickly, along with the resources we used during the sales training program. Even if we did that program a year or two before, all of those resources are still in place for the company's use. Sometimes a manager is ineffective as a coach or doesn't have the time needed to spend with a new hire, so they ask for our help. We have people who know our system and will do one-on-one individual sales coaching with new hires. Similarly, our accountability coaching program helps busy managers by taking over some of their coaching duties and working with a team member who's struggling. Sometimes the manager just needs a one-two punch—a little extra coaching in addition to the work they're doing, so we provide that.

These are just some of the services Intelligent Conversations provides, and within those categories, we probably have nearly a hundred different sales topics we can deploy, depending on the situation. But again, everything we do is highly customized, and we're always creating new content based on different situations I see in the work and on what our clients need. We don't take a one-size-fits-all approach. It's tailored and customized based on what the client needs, and I think that's why we are so successful.

CONCLUSION

IF YOU'RE LIKE most CEOs we've met in our work, you're happy with how most areas in your company are running, but you're frustrated with sales. You're comfortable fixing problems in operations or finance or other areas, but you don't feel like you have the sales team you deserve. You've done step one: you recognize the problem. Step two is knowing you have to do something about it, but you don't know exactly what to do.

You've already read this book, so that's a great start, and if this book is the catalyst for you to start making some changes on your own, that's great. There are plenty of strategies in the book, and I've given you a framework for implementing them. I also provide resources on my website to help you transform your sales team if you decide to go it alone. Visit www.intelligentconversations.com and click on the resources tab to download free white papers on topics that are important to sales team transformation such as personality and behavioral styles assessments, the modern science of selecting salespeople, a sales force evaluation checklist, trade show tips and advice, and much more. I also provide a recommended reading list of must-read books to help you implement the ideas I have outlined in this book. On the tools page, you'll find helpful calculators and graders that will show you, for example, the cost of your hiring mistakes, the relative effectiveness of your sales force, and how much your former salespeople still cost your company, among others. I personally curate and continually update these resources, so visit us often.

If you have been accepting a mediocre sales team rather than the sales team you deserve, what is it costing you in terms of lost revenue? Twenty percent? Thirty percent? More than that? Have you lost market share? Have you given away margin? What's the real cost of your inaction?

My hope is that by reading this book to the very end, you have decided to invest in building a high performing sales culture and will do whatever it takes to get there. You want to follow the science and leverage proven systems that will help you get the high-performing, high-caliber sales team you truly deserve.

If that's the case, please contact us. When you work with Intelligent Conversations, we will make sure that your sales team matches every other part of your company and you no longer have to settle for mediocrity.

If you want to continue the conversation or look into it more deeply, send us an email at mike.carroll@intelligentconversations.com, and we'll take it from there.

ABOUT THE AUTHOR

AS FOUNDER AND MANAGING PARTNER of Intelligent Conversations, Mike Carroll brings more than thirty years of sales and sales leadership experience to his clients. Working hands-on with senior executives, sales leaders, and salespeople, Mike implements programs that change behaviors, grow new skills, and drive remarkable results. Using the proven methodologies described in this book, Mike has worked with hundreds of CEOs and thousands of sales leaders and salespeople to transform sales teams.

Prior to starting Intelligent Conversations in 2004, Mike held senior positions in sales, sales management, and product management at companies including Wachovia Bank (now Wells Fargo), M&I Bank (now BMO Harris), Fiserv, and Mindlever. Mike and his wife Pam have four children and live in Milwaukee, Wisconsin, where they are active community volunteers and foster parents.

CPSIA information can be obtained
at www.ICGtesting.com
Printed in the USA
LVHW081927250322
714381LV00027B/1686

9 780578 384320